# Agility Success

**Training and Competing With Your Dog in the Winning Zone**

by *Angelica Steinker* M. Ed.

35 Walnut Street
Turners Falls, MA 01376

Agility Success
Training and Competing with Your Dog in the Winning Zone

Published by       Clean Run Productions, LLC
                   35 Walnut Street
                   Turners Falls, MA 01376
                   (800) 311-6503 or (413) 863-9243
                   info@cleanrun.com
                   www.cleanrun.com

**Editors** Vicki Hoelzer-Maddox, Betsey Lynch, Linda Mecklenburg, Monica Percival, and Marcille Ripperton
**Cover Design** Carol Stephens
**Book Design and Typesetting** Carol Stephens
**Illustrations** Christine Fain
**Photos** Robyn Broock, Rebecca Cheek, Susan Garrett, Mike Godsil, Pam Hatfield, Anna Jonsson, K9's in Motion, Jane LeGard, Lori Lewis, Ardis Lukens, Duncan McGilvray, Bill Newcomb, Kathy Pepin, Monica Percival, Lynn Sickinger, Skipper Productions (Front Cover), Sue Sternberg, Tien Tran, Mary Wakeman (Back Cover)
**Printing** Hadley Printing Company

First edition
First printing February 2000
United States of America

ISBN 1-892694-03-4

Thank you to my husband, whose help with this book is invisible but immeasurable. I love you infinity squared infinity. Thank you to my mom, who was my most helpful editor, and to my dad for his kind words and encouragement. Also, thank you to: Monica Percival, Linda Mecklenburg, Pati Hatfield, Lori Lewis, Brandy Oliver, Diane Tosh, and all of the competitors for allowing me to interview them. Thank you to Vicki Hoelzer-Maddox for her technical editing. Finally, thank you to my dogs Moose, Junior, Arnie, and Nicki for teaching me to believe in you, and to listen carefully.

*Featuring advice and helpful hints from top competitors, including:*

- KEN BOYD
- ELICIA CALHOUN
- MARQUAND CHEEK
- JULIE DANIELS
- SUSAN GARRETT
- KATIE GREER
- NANCY GYES
- PATI HATFIELD
- BUD HOUSTON
- MINDY LYTLE
- STUART MAH
- LINDA MECKLENBURG
- MONICA PERCIVAL
- JANE SIMMONS-MOAKE
- DIANE TOSH

# Contents

# *Introduction*

This book is about helping you find ways to get into the Zone when you compete in agility. What is the Zone?

The Zone is what we agility enthusiasts are addicted to. Jane Simmons-Moake describes it like this: "*One of the most exciting runs I can remember where Holly and I Zoned was our Team Jumpers run at the 1996 Agility World Championships in Morges, Switzerland. Despite the tremendous noise from cheering spectators and air horns, etc., during our run nothing else existed besides my dog and myself. It felt like we were achieving perfect harmony and teamwork. Never once did I feel like our run was on the edge or that I had slipped into a reactive rather than a proactive mode in my handling. It was over all too soon and I rejoined reality when I crossed the finish line.*"

The Zone, also called *Flow*, according to Csikszentmihalyi (I am not making up this name) "*is a state of concentration so focused that it amounts to absolute absorption in an activity.*" Everyone experiences the Zone from time to time and will recognize its characteristics. "*People typically feel strong, alert, effortless control, unselfconscious and at the peak of their abilities. Both the sense of time and emotional struggles seem to disappear, and there is an exhilarating feeling.*" So the Zone is a pretty cool place to be.

Regardless of whether you are headed for the World Agility Championships or for a clean run in a Novice agility class, this book can help you enter your winning Zone.

Jane Simmons-Moake and Holly trying to achieve the same perfect harmony and teamwork at the 1997 Agility World Championships in Denmark that they experienced in 1996 in Switzerland.

When you enter the Zone it means that things are clicking. Everything is falling into place. When we begin to learn to run courses with our dogs, we have moments in the Zone; moments when everything clicks into place.

Different people experience the Zone in different ways. Stuart Mah describes how he experiences Zoning: "*A Zone run definitely feels like time is moving in slow motion. You are so focused and concentrating so hard on your run and on the dog that it seems like the run cannot possibly be as fast as the recorded time says it is. You are aware of everything that your dog and you do, but you are not necessarily aware of anything else around you, like the judge, people, or the crowd. The year that my dog Shannon won the USDAA National title I could not figure out why she had such a spurt of speed after the weave poles. It was not until I saw the videotape of the run that I heard the crowd urging her on with their cheering. I truly never heard it, but yet, I was acutely aware of the judge's count on the table. In a Zone run, you basically turn off or tune out everything that is not absolutely essential for the perfect run.*"

While Jane and Stuart both describe a state of heightened concentration in which they were able to effortlessly block out all other noises and distractions, Stuart experienced a slowing of time while he was Zoning. This is an example of how individual Zone experiences are.

Although the top competitors interviewed for this book all experienced the Zone differently, they consistently described feeling as if they were one with the dog, or a sense of being free.

Julie Daniels spoke of the feeling of oneness. "*I have had a number of Zone runs over the years, and they are fundamentally different from other clean runs. Before a Zone run, I still get that twinge of nerves as I walk to the start line. Then suddenly I am comfortable and eager again, breathing calmly and enjoying being beside my wonderful dog. I love the course. It belongs to us. As we begin, I have a perfect feel for where the obstacles are all around me, and my dog and I navigate smoothly. My dog knows what I am thinking. Though my overall plan is clear to me, I am thinking only one second at a time, obstacle by obstacle. The dog seems to be going on my will and focus alone. I hear nothing but my own focus, and I think of nothing but my great dog and the steps through the course. The course feels familiar the first time through. When we are in the Zone together, the wrong obstacles do not exist. The only thing next is the correct thing. We focus on what we want and we do it together. That is all there is; no extraneous thought, no worry, and no hesitation. The connection is powerful. Afterward comes the rush that we made the course look and feel so easy.*"

Susan Garrett described the Zone like this: "*One recent weekend that comes to mind is the USDAA Grand Prix regional qualifier held in Lexington, Kentucky at the end of April. Traditionally this is a tough weekend for us because it is the first run of the season. Being from Canada, our winter/spring weather often prevents us from getting a chance to run any courses at all for five months prior to coming down to the Kentucky trial. Nonetheless, we always try to attend this trial as the venue is gorgeous, and it is great to start the season by visiting with so many old friends. Plus many of the top handlers are there. This year was no different as the competition was tough and we were rusty (not having run a course since November).*

When Stuart Mah is Zoning, he is unaware of the crowd and other distractions around him. The ability to concentrate only on the dog and the course is an important factor in success, especially at major events like the Agility World Championships. Here are Stuart and his Border Collie Recce at the 1999 World Championships in Germany.

PHOTO BY ANNA JONSSON.

Susan Garrett recalls a weekend where her Jack Russell Terrier Twister was working in a different "Zone" than Susan, and reminds us that the less than spectacular runs are the ones that make the good runs feel so much better.

PHOTO BY TIEN TRAN.

*I must admit the three dogs and I did have some runs that were less than spectacular, but those are the ones that make the really good runs feel so much better. Your highs are always highest if you have had to struggle to get there. In the end Shelby won the Steeplechase final (in the 12-inch division) and Stoni won the Grand Prix (in the 24-inch division). Both of these runs were definitely in 'the Zone.' We did have one or two others during the weekend that hit as well, where we ended up with 5 faults. That is okay too. Having a 'Zoned' run has nothing to do with what place we end up in, but everything to do with how well we work together as a team. A knocked bar is going to happen on occasion, but that will not affect how good I feel about how we worked together as a team. My Jack Russell Terrier Twister was in a Zone all weekend too, but I think it was the Twilight Zone. Here is a dog that cannot get by with six months away from agility!!!*

*When I think back on these and other runs 'in the Zone,' what hits me is how fast these runs were over. It seems as if I am just setting up at the start line and in a blink of an eye we have crossed the finish line. My dog reacts to my directives as if it is the tenth or eleventh time we have run the course. It is the true definition of teamwork. I feel as if we could keep going for another 40 obstacles. It is almost as if the two of us are attached somehow. These runs seem to happen more frequently as the dog gets more experience running courses and I get more experience with the individual needs of each dog that I run.*"

If you are just starting out in agility, you may need to think of other accomplishments in order to get clear on how the Zone feels to you. Recall a time where everything flowed. How about the time in school you were bombarded with questions and had every answer? Or the time you nailed that presentation at work? These moments were when you performed your best—you were in the Zone!

The goal of this book is to help you train the mental skills needed to consistently recreate peak agility performances and therefore be Zoning. Recreate that day when you and your dog ran every course clean; that run when everything came together. Imagine having that virtually every time you compete. You can. All it takes is some practice. Using the techniques described, you can consistently perform in the Zone.

## Chapter 1

# *Getting Into the Zone*

*"Once you are physically capable of winning a gold medal, the rest is 90% mental."*

—Patti Johnson, Olympic Hurdler

Okay, here is the deal: to get into the Zone every individual needs to make specific things happen. When these things occur, you Zone. When they do not, you do not. The cool fact is that you can make these things happen and therewith make the Zone happen. Let us call these things natural laws since they are like the natural phenomenon of gravity. You cannot argue with gravity, it just is. The 11 natural laws of Zoning are like that, they just are.

## The 11 Natural Laws of Zoning

Susan Garrett says: *"Be aware of what role you play in your dog's mistakes. Do not blame your dog for an off-course or missed contact. Our dogs are only a reflection of us. Any weaknesses our dogs have are not theirs and theirs alone, these weaknesses are only reflections of our weaknesses as a trainer or handler. Any area where your dog is less skilled, is an area where you have limitations as a dog trainer. So work harder on improving your own abilities and only look for what is good about your dog. This will help you come to the start line with more confidence. Never lose sight of the fact that regardless of what goes on in the ring, these guys are still primarily our pets who we will love no matter what."*

1. **Always take responsibility for the errors your dog makes.** When you take responsibility for your dog's errors, you can control them. If you blame the dog, you are saying you have no control over the error and can therefore not solve it. So if your dog gets sucked into the tunnel, you say, "That was my error for not practicing more tunnel traps."

2. **Believe in your dog.** Believe the dog has the ability to do what you are asking of her. When you believe in your dog, you trust her. If you do not believe in your dog, your dog will not perform at her peak. Ken Boyd says that he and others did not really believe that Becky could compete at the level that she did. He explains that he and the others were not being negative, they felt they were being realistic. However, as Ken continued training with Becky he began to think that she could do *"very, very well,"* because she was both fast and accurate. Although some of his fellow competitors commented that they did not think that a Corgi could pull off multiple national wins, in the back of his mind, Ken continued to believe in Becky. In 1997 Becky the Corgi became the first dog in agility history to win all three national finals (and she did it in the same year): AKC, NADAC, and USDAA.

3. **Have fun.** If you do not have fun you will find yourself outside of the Zone. Not having fun can also lead to handler burnout and to doggie burnout.

4. **Care for yourself like you care for your dog.** Eat right. Get enough rest. Do what you have to so that you can be comfortable training and competing.

5. **Practice the physical skills required for you to succeed.** Having the physical skills will give you confidence.

6. **Practice the mental skills required for you to succeed.** Know what mental skills you need to practice and then as the Nike ads exclaim, "Just do it."

7. **Teach yourself to focus on command.** Training for focus is a crucial element of zoning.

8. **Wear "positive everything sunglasses."** When you put on positive everything sunglasses, everything you see and experience has a positive spin on it.

9. **Praise your dog.** Praising your dog has a magical effect on you.

10. **Relax your body.** A tense mind cannot exist in a relaxed body.

11. **Implement your pre-competition ritual.** More about this later.

The laws listed above are true for all agility handlers, but each of us has to find those natural laws that are most important for us to get into the Zone. That is what this book is all about, helping *you* find *your* natural laws for Zoning. Use the 11 laws previously listed as a beginning for creating your own list of factors that get you into the Zone.

NOTE: If you are a novice competitor and have not experienced a Zone run, think of the times that you Zoned in other areas of your life. What were the factors that made the Zoning happen? Use these factors to help you brainstorm what might work for you in agility.

**My Zone factors are**

Using your list of Zone factors will help you get into the Zone. Please reevaluate your list periodically.

## What Keeps You From Getting into the Zone?

On the left is a graph that depicts the Zone. The trick to consistently performing in the Zone is finding strategies that allow you to be in the proper *arousal state*. Arousal state refers to how excited you are about what you are doing. If you are too aroused (too excited), your performance will suffer. Likewise, if you are not aroused enough (not excited), your performance will also suffer. So Zoning is a balancing act. You want to be excited—just not too excited.

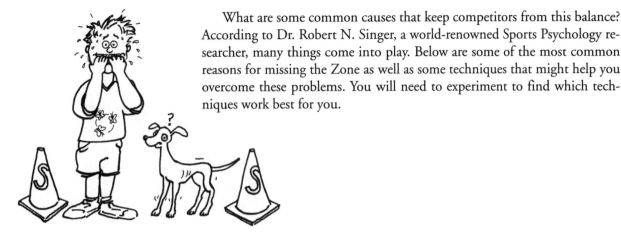

What are some common causes that keep competitors from this balance? According to Dr. Robert N. Singer, a world-renowned Sports Psychology researcher, many things come into play. Below are some of the most common reasons for missing the Zone as well as some techniques that might help you overcome these problems. You will need to experiment to find which techniques work best for you.

Is your arousal state too high? Are you nervous and need to relax to do your best?

### Most Common Causes for Being Too Excited in Competition

- **Outcome uncertainty.** You are not confident about what will happen and are very nervous.

  SOLUTION: Read the chapters on Confidence and Thought Power. These chapters discuss techniques and ideas for building confidence and thinking positively.

- **Meaningfulness of event.** You are nervous because this is a big competition.

  SOLUTION: Go and watch big competitions ahead of time so that you will be familiar with how these events run. Be *overprepared* for what will be required of you and your dog.

- **Fear of failing or of looking bad.** You are nervous because you are worried about not succeeding or about being embarrassed. You may also feel this way if you have entered your dog into competition before she has learned all of the necessary skills.

  SOLUTION: Be overprepared. Jane Simmons-Moake does not allow her students to compete until they are training at a Masters level and they are willing to bet money that they have a good shot at winning their class.

- **Fear of letting down significant others.** Worrying about letting down a significant other, family member, friend, or trainer can also cause nervousness. Running someone else's dog can also cause this problem.

  SOLUTION: Building confidence, evaluating and changing your thinking, and many other things suggested in this book will help you guard against this.

- **Fear of danger.** You might be afraid of injuring yourself or your dog and this could cause you to be nervous. This also applies when you are recovering from an injury to either you or your dog. The fear of re-injury can cause nerves to soar.

  SOLUTION: If either you or your dog is recovering from an injury, do not enter a competition too soon. Take your time and compete when you are ready. Never compete on equipment or under conditions that you consider unsafe.

- **Intimidation of opponent.** Let us hope that this is not applicable to agility; however, a fellow agility competitor might intimidate another handler without even intending to. For example, suppose a competitor has just moved up to the AKC Excellent level and finds out that she will be competing against a member of the World Team. This could easily cause the less-experienced competitor to feel intimidated and get nervous.

  SOLUTION: Build your confidence and be overprepared.

- **Unfamiliarity.** Anything that you or the dog might be unfamiliar with will cause nervousness and could bump you out of the Zone. This can include many things such as the physical environment (show site), the equipment, and even the weather.

  SOLUTION: Prepare for as many different situations as you can. Expose yourself and your dog to as many different show sites and running conditions as possible.

- **Unexpected events.** A sudden change in running order or anything unexpected can cause a surge of show nerves.

  SOLUTION: Learn to expect the unexpected.

Competitors who tend to struggle with getting too excited have explained that they prevent this by pretending that the pending competition run is just practice. By fooling themselves into believing they are about to practice, these competitors have had great success in avoiding a huge onset of show nerves. Just pretend it is practice.

Is your arousal state too low? Do you need to get more excited to do your best?

## Most Common Causes for Not Being Excited Enough in Competition

- **Certainty of winning.** An overconfident handler does not get excited enough. The resulting blasé attitude will have a wet-blanket effect on the performance.

  SOLUTION: Explore the reason behind your overconfidence. Look at what needs to happen for you to get more motivated and try a little harder.

- **Certainty of losing.** Apathy and/or pessimistic thinking can cause low arousal.

  SOLUTION: Develop new ways of thinking. Read the chapter on Thought Power.

- **Bored.** Long-time competitors may feel a lack of sufficient challenge and as a result will not handle to the best of their abilities.

  SOLUTION: Find a new challenge in agility. Start a new dog. Take a break from agility so that it will be fun again. Start another dog sport for variety.

JANE SIMMONS-MOAKE describes an example of how she avoided low arousal from being a factor in an important performance at the 1996 World Championships, *"When I initially saw the course laid out I was concerned, not about its difficulty but about the incredibly wide (30- to 40-foot) spacing between each of the obstacles. In the States, we do not typically see courses with this amount of spacing throughout. I told myself that the course would be a challenge, but with Holly's excellent distance skills we could pull it off if I remained alert and in control of the situation. I have found that it is important for me not to become overconfident. Even if the course appears relatively simple, I convince myself that it will be a challenge and that I need to work hard throughout the entire run."*

If Jane had allowed herself to become overconfident, her arousal state would have been too low and she would not have had a Zone run. Fortunately, Jane was aware of this dynamic and immediately guarded against it.

- **Lack of confidence in handling ability or in the dog's training.** A handler who thinks that a course is too hard or that her dog cannot do the course will have trouble getting excited.

  SOLUTION: Be overprepared. Make sure you have practiced at a higher level than what you will encounter.

- **Negative self-talk.** A negative handler will not be able to get excited enough for a Zone run. If you are interested in sabotaging your performance, try negative self-talk.

  SOLUTION: Stop it. Start noticing when you are having a negative thought. When you notice a negative thought, turn it into a game where you must substitute it with two positive thoughts.

- **Burnout.** A burned-out handler is not likely to get excited enough to achieve a Zone run.

  SOLUTION: Consider what has been helpful to you in the past, if you burned out in other situations. Take a break. Do non-agility things in your life. Read a novel. Find the fun again.

- **Depression.** If you or someone you know is depressed, it is important to seek professional assistance. Apathy, lack of appetite or an overly high appetite, sleeping too much, not being able to concentrate, and an inability to free yourself from negative thoughts, can all be signs of depression.

  SOLUTION: Get in touch with a professional who can assist you in taking the steps necessary to break the depression cycle.

## Getting Your Dog into the Zone

Besides getting yourself in the Zone, you have to get your dog into the Zone. The first step to getting your dog into the Zone is to know your dog. For each of the categories below, list what your dog likes. What your dog likes is your ticket to motivation and to building a great relationship with your dog.

- **Play.** What type of play does she like? If she likes more than one type of play, which one is her favorite? Resist the temptation to answer that your dog likes all games. Be specific in your response. The more specific you are, the more useful the information will be.

- **Food.** What type of food does she like? List her favorite food rewards below. Begin with the most favorite. Again, be as specific as you can.

<br>
<br>
<br>

- **Toy.** What type of toy is your dog's favorite? Why do you think she likes it so much? List all of your dog's favorite toys below.

<br>
<br>
<br>

- **Touch.** How does your dog like to be touched? On which parts of her body does she like to be touched the most? Does she like soft touch, vigorous massaging, or does she like to be scratched?

<br>
<br>
<br>

- **Praise.** What type of praise makes your dog the happiest? Does she like a soft voice or does she like loud cheering with arms waving?

<br>
<br>
<br>

Out of the rewards listed above, which one is your dog's first choice? This is what your dog would consider the ultimate reward. You can be creative and mix items from several categories. Describe your dog's ultimate reward below:

<br>
<br>
<br>

Since you have the information on what your dog likes most, you can now put this to work in your training. The top competitors know nothing better than their own dogs. Mindy Lytle carries a little swimming pool complete with rubber duckies to every show because she knows that her dog Zoe really likes to have a swim. Knowing what your dog likes, helps you get your dog into her Zone.

When working with the rewards listed above, it is extremely important to learn to use and emphasize physical touch and praise the most. Praise is not something dogs enjoy naturally. Since dogs do not understand your words, praise could be totally meaningless to them. However, dogs learn that praise means good things will happen, or that when you praise them, you are happy and that means they are more likely to get something that they want. Eventually the praise itself will become fun to the dog. Teaching your dog that praise is wonderful is one of the most important elements of bonding with your dog.

Especially if you have an independent breed, you need to teach your dog to work for praise and love rubs. In most cases it will take the independent dogs more time to learn this. You can speed up their learning by pairing their favorite food reward, say liver, with physical touch and praise. Praise your dog, give her a great butt rub, and then feed the liver. Repeat this every time you reward your dog. Eventually the praise and rubs will be just as powerful as the liver.

What would you rather be to your dog, a food dispenser or a supplier of the world's best praise and butt rubs? Agility is about your relationship with your dog: love you take into the ring with you, food waits at the gate.

Consider that when you are using physical and verbal praise you can prolong the reward process for as long as you like. Suddenly, five minutes of reward time is a possibility. A food reward lasts only as long as the dog chews, that is, if she even chews. The only other reward that you can draw out over minutes is play. That is why tugging has such a powerful effect when used as a reward for agility training.

Finally, the most important aspect of knowing your dog is being aware of her physical health. Marq Cheek says, *"I was caught unaware on my first competition dog (Thomas) when his performances began to diminish over a series of months. We had a wonderful rapport, his diet was very good, and he seemed healthy. It was not until he ultimately became lame that I finally had him analyzed by a vet and subsequently an orthopedic surgeon. It was discovered, via a nuclear imaging scan (bone scintigraphy), that he had a jammed little toe that was not healing. I feel awful about that incident, but it taught me a very important lesson: get in tune with your dog and be sensitive to even the slightest degradation in performance."*

An important book regarding the dog and his athletic performance was written by Dr. Chris Zink. *Peak Performance: Coaching the Canine Athlete* is a must-read for any serious agility competitor and will give you a good base of knowledge about canine structure and the most common canine sports injuries.

## Questions to Ask Yourself

| 1. In the past, in what situations have you and/or your dog been too excited? | |
|---|---|

| 2. What happened during the times you were not excited enough? | |
|---|---|

| 3. List the factors that cause you to be too excited: | |
|---|---|

| 4. Now list what you can do to combat each of these factors: | |
|---|---|

| 5. List what factors have caused you to not be excited enough: | |
|---|---|

| 6. Now list what you can do for each of the factors that caused you to not be excited: | |
|---|---|

# Chapter 2

# Goal Setting

*Without goals, you are like a dog on course without a handler.*
*You lack direction.*

Goals! They can be fun. They can mean pressure. They can be boring. They can be too challenging. They can be just right and get you exactly what you want. When you set goals, you need to gather information to make sure that you are setting goals that will impact you and your dog in a positive way. Consider all the suggestions below so that you can set goals that get you into your Zone.

### Have a dream.

By having a dream you are creating a mental focal point. If you do not have a dream, it will be much more difficult for you to focus and effectively set small goals. Make sure that your dream does not accidentally become a goal. The difference between a dream and a goal is that you can control the outcome of the goal. You cannot control whether your dream comes true or not.

For example, if you dream of going to the Nationals, do not make that your goal. Rather, use the dream of the Nationals to help you focus on the process of what you need to do to get to the Nationals. By focusing on the small steps of improving your handling, and other such steps, you can make your dream become a reality. For instance, set a goal such as: "I am going to give all my commands early." This way you are setting a goal of focusing on the process that is going to improve your handling and ultimately can help make your dream of reaching the Nationals come true.

### Set daily and weekly goals that are stepping stones to your dream.

This type of goal setting breaks the dream down into smaller, more manageable tasks. Here is an example.

*Dream:* Nationals

*Daily Goal:* During my daily practice, I will call the next obstacle as my dog is completing the current obstacle. On days when I am unable to practice or my dog needs a day off, I will practice this mentally by visualizing the dog performing obstacles and myself giving commands early.

Ken Boyd's biggest goal is to finish a course and have Becky give him that look of "Hey, dad, that was really fun!" Achieving that goal on numerous occasions led Ken and Becky not only to the 1997 12-inch AKC Agility Championship, but to a win in the 12-inch division at the 1997 USDAA and NADAC National Championships as well.

<small>PHOTO BY K9'S IN MOTION.</small>

*Weekly Goal:* Once a week, I will videotape a run and then review how many obstacles I called early. For each five obstacles I called early, I will reward myself with _____. (This could be a music CD, a yummy snack, a TV show, entries to an agility trial, or nothing because the activity itself may have been rewarding to you.)

To continue progress toward your dream of the Nationals it will be important to reevaluate and change your daily and weekly goals on at least a monthly basis.

### Do not allow yourself to be bothered when you miss a goal.

You should write goals in pencil. Reaching your goals is a journey, not a two-step process of writing down the goal and realizing it.

*Example:* I reviewed my weekly video and I only called three obstacles early. My goal was calling at least five obstacles early. I am going to have a friend come by and help me practice by calling early for me, so that I can hear when I need to be calling the obstacles.

### Challenge yourself.

A challenge is a situation where you push yourself, but are likely to succeed because most factors are in your favor. Do not set yourself up to fail. If distraction is an issue for you, set up distractions to test your concentration. If you know that it is harder for you to concentrate when you are nervous, deliberately expose yourself to lots of situations in which you are nervous. Remember, these situations do not need to involve agility, you could be at the dentist's office waiting to get your tooth drilled and be practicing your concentration.

*Example:* When I have been doing sequences, I have been successful giving commands early for up to seven obstacles. This week my instructor will set up a 12-obstacle course and I plan to run the entire course calling all obstacles early.

### Patience.

Just because a goal has been set does not mean that the desired result will just appear. Agility training is very hard work. Some dogs are easier to train than others. Either way, you will need to be patient if you are not able to meet goals as rapidly as you would like. Frequently we are able to be very patient with our dogs, but when it comes to being patient with ourselves because we have not mastered a certain handling move, we have no patience. Instead of allowing yourself to become frustrated, use that energy to be patient and eventually you will meet the goal you set.

Ken Boyd and Becky focusing only on running the course as fast as they can in the 1997 USDAA Grand Prix Finals.

PHOTO BY DUNCAN MCGILVRAY.

## Basic Goal Setting

STUART MAH's advice to competitors regarding goal setting: *"Concentrate on being the best and doing your best each time. Setting a goal of winning every time at all costs is unrealistic and can be very self-defeating since it is a goal that can be very difficult to attain. Setting a goal too high can result in frustration and actually bring down the level of the performance. On the other hand, consistently setting a goal of just wanting to get by all the time is just as bad since the level is too low. Setting a low performance standard often leads to poor or mediocre performances. Ideally, a person should set a goal and then constantly reevaluate the goal to see if it's being met. He can then adjust accordingly, the emphasis being on gradually pushing up the goals to higher levels. For example, it is not good for a new handler and dog to expect to win a national title. However, it may be a perfectly adequate goal to just qualify. Maybe the next time the goal should be to be in the finals, not just to qualify. In other words, keep reevaluating your goals and adjust. Never be completely satisfied with just getting by."*

Without goals, you are like a dog on a course without a handler. You lack direction. Setting goals puts you, the handler, back in the ring. The process of setting and pursuing goals can be fun. It can make your agility dreams come true.

- **A goal is a choice that you make.** It is a request. It is not a "should." It is not a failure, and you are not "bad" if you miss a goal. Agility is a process of working toward your goals. Our goals cannot dictate our feelings of satisfaction because we are not reaching goals every day. Likewise, missing a goal should not cause disappointment but rather reevaluation.

- **Enjoy the process.** Take pleasure in deciding what you want to achieve in agility by setting and pursuing goals. Do not worry and obsess about making or not making the goal. Agility is fun, right? Keep your goals fun. If the goal is not fun, change it.

- **Set short-, medium-, and long-range goals.** You can define these time elements any way you wish: short may be one day or several days. Set specific dates if possible. This will help you know when it is time to reevaluate.

- **Be specific.** "I want to train my dog to run up and over the A-frame and then pause at the bottom" is a specific goal and is better than a vague goal like "I want him to do it right." "Right," by not being defined, is too vague and therefore not a good goal. When you are specific, it allows you to accurately track your progress. Breaking this goal into smaller tasks is also a good idea. In terms of the contact performance, you could give yourself the task of teaching your dog to target and then backchaining the performance.

- **Rank goals by their importance and achievability.** Some are important and some may just be fun. Do not limit yourself with easy or mundane goals. Prioritizing your training and competition goals can be tremendously helpful in terms of deciding which goal to begin working on first. The most important goal gets worked on first, and then less important goals follow.

## Goal Setting as a Roadblock to Success

Some people do not enjoy the process of goal setting. They do not enjoy even hearing the word "goal." If this sounds like you, consider swapping the phrase "goal setting" with the phrase "problem solving." Bob Biehl has written an entire book on how some people despise goal setting and love to solve problems instead. In his book, *Stop Setting Goals, If You Would Rather Solve Problems*, he discusses in detail how for some people the goal setting process is de-motivating and about as much fun as poking needles in their eyes. If this seems like you, focus on solving problems or meeting challenges or whatever you want to call it instead. If that is not working, do something different!

For other competitors, goals can be destructive. A goal can create an expectation. An expectation creates a desire. When you have a desire, you get into "must have" mode and this can set you up for disappointment. The bottom line is that you cannot control everything. If you focus on fun, which you can control, you will be much less likely to be disappointed.

As Stuart previously describes, good goal setting is a balance between challenging yourself and not asking too much of yourself or your dog. If you have a tendency to ask too much, try lowering your expectations. This will create less pressure and more fun. What torture! For example, if you do not expect to qualify, you will not be disappointed when you do not. And, if you do qualify, it will be a pleasant surprise.

If for some reason you are disappointed about your performance, do not allow yourself to wallow in it. Marinating is only for cooking, not for your feelings. Marinating in feelings and making excuses is not going to help anyone enter the Zone.

Truly, it only makes sense to have high expectations about things that you can control 100%. What are the things in your life that you have 100% control over? Your car? Well, yes, but not if it breaks unexpectedly. Your dog? Most certainly not. Anyone who trains agility knows that nothing you teach a dog is 100% in every situation. The things you can control mostly have to do with you—your attitude, your thoughts, your behavior, how much you practice. Those are the best things to which to connect your expectations.

Remember the time that your dog left the ring to steal a hot dog out of a kid's hand? You were at the start line ready to go. Your dog was fired up and

If you dream of going to the Nationals, you need to focus on the process of what needs to be done to get to the Nationals. The 1997 USDAA Grand Prix of Dog Agility champions are all handler and dog teams that have focused on improving their handling skills and their dogs' performance skills each year: Pati Hatfield and Lilly, Linda Mecklenburg and Spiffy, Kathie Leggett and Spirit, and Ken Boyd and Becky.

PHOTO BY ROBYN BROOCK.

looking at you. You were feeling connected to your dog and within a split second you were alone in the ring staring at the second obstacle in shock, wondering where your dog went. Hot dogs happen! It is better to laugh about the mishap. After all, you just gained valuable information. Apparently you need to train your dog to resist hot dogs while on the course. This reaction is much more productive than simply engulfing yourself in the misery of one blown run.

Have high expectations only about things you can absolutely control. Expect to have fun *no matter what* happens in the ring. Expect to smile and praise your dog for what she did well *no matter what* happens in the ring.

Whatever method of accomplishment you choose to use, goals or problem solving or whatever else, be sure to be flexible. Things change, so what you are working on must also change. Jump heights change, your dog's age changes, your wishes in terms of what you want to accomplish change, and so on. Setting goals or problem solving should always be done with a pencil and a big eraser!

### Process versus Result

When setting goals it is important to focus on the process of how you are going to make a goal happen. This means that rather than focusing on the result, such as getting to the Nationals, a winning handler focuses on the process—"How am I going to get there?" The winning handler asks herself "What actions do I need to take to make going to the Nationals happen?"

Results you cannot control. Process you can control. This means that every process goal must pass the control test. If you cannot control the outcome, then it is not an ideal goal because you do not really have control over it.

Consider the goal that Stuart mentioned of winning all your classes. This is a shining, gleaming, and alluring goal. However, you cannot control the performance of your competitors. You cannot control equipment failure. You cannot control your dog (not totally 100% of the time). Therefore, it is a result goal and *not* necessarily a good goal. A better goal would be to focus on one particular handling skill such as using a front cross at the tunnel. Or setting several handler goals throughout the course like smiling at your dog, going deep on all turns, and executing all your side changes.

### Example

*Goal:* Going to the Nationals. (Result-oriented goal—Not good)

*Do you have 100% control?* No, many things could prevent this from happening. Dog could get sick. You could make handling errors and miss qualifying.

*New Goal:* Do the best that I can every time I go in the ring. Have fun and praise my dog. Focus on smooth handling and giving my dog clear signals. (Process-oriented goal—Excellent!)

List some goals that you currently have. Then indicate whether you have control over making them happen. Reword each goal that you do not have control over until it is a process goal.

List your goals:

 

Do you have 100% control of each goal?

 

If not, what are your new process-oriented goals?

 

Here are some examples of other process-oriented goals:

- I will stop my training sessions with my dog before she wants to stop.
- I will focus on my relationship with my dog in training and in competition.
- While warming up my dog, I will play with my dog for at least five minutes.
- When I reward my dog for a good performance, I will play with her for at least five minutes.
- I will smile at my dog while we are in the ring.
- I will stay with my dog while in the ring. I will not lead out (because she is not ready for it) and I will not get ahead of her.
- I will laugh and smile in the ring no matter what happens.

Mindy Lytle tries to only set training goals rather than specific goals for her runs. This allows her to always focus on the process and what she's learning. Here is Mindy's Jack Russell Terrier, Zoe.

PHOTO BY TIEN TRAN.

Ken Boyd's example of a process goal is to focus on running as fast and as well as he and Becky can. His biggest goal is to finish the course and to have Becky give him that look of "Hey, dad, that was really fun!" Both of Ken's goals are wonderful examples of process goals.

If you are confused about the difference between a result-oriented goal and a process-oriented goal, there is a simple way to make sure you are focusing on a process goal. Mindy Lytle developed this technique and it is very simple: "*Focus on what you are learning.*"

### What Do You Control?

The following list shows some of the things you can control in competition and some you cannot control.

| Controllable | Uncontrollable |
| --- | --- |
| Your behavior | Others' attitudes, thoughts, emotions and behavior |
| Your physical condition | Other competitors' performances |
| Your motivation/effort | Your trainer/coach |
| Your attitude | Your family |
| Your thoughts | Timers, ring stewards, and judges |
| Your emotions | Whom you are competing against in your class |
| Your clothing | Competition conditions |
| Your preparation | Weather |

What things can you add to this list?

| Controllable | Uncontrollable |
| --- | --- |
| | |
| | |
| | |

Mindy Lytle has made it a habit to only set goals in situations where she has control. She recommends setting training goals, but not having any specific goals for your runs. If she does have a goal for her run, it will center on trying out new handling techniques. If the technique goes well, great, and if it does not, she will focus on what she learned. Mindy is setting herself up for a win/win.

### Solutions to Potential Problems When Goal Setting

Continue experimenting until you find the method that is ideal for you. Each person is different and requires different types of goal setting.

Monitoring the goals and adjusting them is most important. Sports psychology research shows that goal setting becomes ineffective when you do not monitor and readjust your goals.

Finally, do not set too many goals from the start. If you enjoy goal setting and it has been effective for you, resist the temptation of setting more goals than you can work on in a week.

### Handler Rewards

One way to avoid problems when setting goals is to use rewards. As trainers, we know to reward our dogs. We know that no dog would do agility on her own, but that we have to teach her the required behavior and then reward the desired performance. As instructors and students we need to learn to reward desired behavior in people.

Keep in mind that rewards are very subjective. Just as each dog is different and motivated by different things, each person has different preferences.

Here are some ideas for handler rewards:

- Verbal praise
- Acknowledgment of desired behavior in front of others
- A piece of candy
- A professional massage
- A book or magazine subscription
- Entries to a show
- A piece of agility equipment

The list above is especially important for instructors. Teaching agility can be frustrating. Focusing on what your students are doing right, and rewarding it, is more fun.

If you are an instructor, never underestimate the power of praising your students. Especially if you are frustrated with a student, praise for every little thing the student does correctly and see the frustration melt away. Focus on the positive and you will get more of it.

Whether you are teaching or just learning, the goal of reward training is to make the activity itself rewarding or self-reinforcing. Once you have learned how to handle a tough sequence, running the sequence successfully will become the actual reward. For the instructor, seeing the students successfully tackle a tough sequence is the ultimate compliment.

So, what do you enjoy?

I enjoy

I like to eat

I like to listen to

I like to be told

I like to be praised by

I like to feel

Share what you have written above with the friends you train with and with your instructor. All of us instinctively reward other people as we would want to be rewarded. One agility competitor told me she really likes to get prizes. For example, she would enjoy the reward of getting a Beanie Baby toy. If this competitor does not tell the people she trains with this is the type of reward she enjoys, they might reward her with a box of toffee, which has little effect on her.

## Goal Setting in Competition

SUSAN GARRETT describes how she sets goals in competition: *"Too many handlers leave the ring feeling dejected as they did not qualify. Set small goals before entering a competition that are not just 'getting a leg.' It is too easy to feel disappointed in your dog and in yourself, and you will soon lose the spirit of competing. Set a smaller goal such as hitting all of your up contacts or having your dog wait at the start line or something else you have been working on. Have a list that you can look back on and say 'Well I did not get a leg, but we did do this, this, and this.' This is how you can take a positive feeling away from each run."*

Note how Susan is recommending that you set yourself up for success by focusing on accomplishing only a small goal that has been well trained.

Susan Garrett's focus on setting small goals in competition has ultimately led to big wins. Here she is (left) with her Jack Russell Terrier Shelby, winner of the 8-inch division at the 1999 Pup-Peroni Agility Championship. Her JRT Twister took the 12-inch division at the event.

PHOTO BY MIKE GODSIL.

## Questions to Ask Yourself

| | |
|---|---|
| **1. In the past, what types of goals have worked for you?** | |
| **2. What did these goals have in common?** | |
| **3. In the past, what goals have not worked for you?** | |
| **4. Do you dislike the term goal setting? If yes, try changing "goal setting" to "problem solving" or to "challenge." What would you rather call goal setting?** | |
| **5. If a goal is not working for you, have you checked if you can really control the outcome of this goal?** | |

If you cannot control the outcome, it is time to reword or change the goal to focus on something that you *can* control.

Goal setting is like teaching a dog how to weave through a set of poles. You have to break down the behavior into small pieces and make it easy for the dog to succeed; otherwise the dog will dislike the weave poles. Notice that the small behaviors must be things the dog can control. Asking the dog for a specific behavior that she cannot control would be a waste of time. Part of the training process for weave poles is to set up the dog to succeed by making each step of the training controllable, fun, and easy. This is how goal setting should be done. Just call it shaping for people. You are breaking your own behavior down into small pieces, the mini goals, so that you can accomplish a big goal (weaving 12 poles).

| | |
|---|---|
| **6. What is your new goal that you can control?** | |
| **7. List your mini goals in order of importance. You will begin working on the most important mini goal and then build on that.** | |

Make sure your mini goals include training goals and a commitment to how many days a week and minutes per training session. Without setting aside the time that it takes to practice, it is impossible to achieve anything.

Now use your goal and the mini goals as a map to guide you in your journey into the Zone.

### Goal Shrinking and Stretching

Use the area below to experiment with goal shrinking and stretching. If the goal is overwhelming, shrink it. If it is not challenging, stretch it. Once you have practiced this in training, the skill will be very useful in competition. If the course seems too easy, for example, you will have practiced "stretching" your goals so that you can make it seem harder. If the course seems too challenging, you can set a goal around a certain sequence that will help you "shrink" the challenge of the course. Remember that the goals you set have the ability to help you get into the Zone or knock you right out of it.

Describe a very big goal that you have. An example would be qualifying for the Nationals or the World Championships.

MACH - TORCH

Now shrink this goal by breaking it down into smaller, mini goals that all help you work toward the big goal. Make sure the mini goals are all process goals.

KEEP RUNS QUIET
KEEP ARMS UNDER CONTROL
CONTACTS

Describe a very small goal that is not interesting to you (you will not be motivated to try to achieve this goal, because it is too small). An example might be making smooth turns in a pinwheel of jumps when you are consistently making smooth turns in all your runs.

LAYERING THREE JUMPS

Now, take this unchallenging goal and stretch it so that it becomes challenging to you. An example would be a making smooth *and tight* turns in a pinwheel of jumps.

LAYERING JUMPS WITH A SMOOTH TURN AT THE END

The previous example should make it clear why it is a good idea to set goals using a pencil. Goals must change and adapt all the time. Whenever a change occurs, it is time for a "goal workout" of stretching and shrinking! As your handling skills improve, your goals will need to change.

## Goal Setting and Motivation

*"The marvelous richness of human experience would lose something of rewarding joy if there were no limitations to overcome. The hilltop hour would not be half so wonderful if there were no dark valleys to traverse."*

—HELEN KELLER

Usually it is not a struggle to define the dream. Competitors are easily motivated to think or talk about their dream. The challenge is to find the daily motivation to do tasks that lead to the realization of that dream.

When you examine people and how they are motivated, you find information that sounds like dog training! Just consider the following information presented by Dr. Robert Singer, Professor and Researcher at the University of Florida, at an American Psychological Association Conference on the topic of Sports Psychology.

The following are typical approaches to motivation (behavioral):

1. Rewards

2. Punishment—that sounds fun (pardon the sarcasm)

3. Bribes—another great one

4. Threats—this one is even better

5. Recognition

Out of the above, which ones would motivate you? One and five are obviously the most pleasant, so the truth is that you need to motivate yourself as you do your dog. If you lose the fun, you are likely to lose the motivation.

Bud Houston recommends that competitors stay motivated by reminding themselves "*This is only a game that is FUN and play for the entire family. Do not take it seriously.*" Taking agility too seriously can greatly hamper your motivation to train and eventually to compete.

To be properly motivated, you will require reinforcement just as your dog does. When you are feeling a lack of motivation, a good first step is to explore where you usually get your reinforcement. If winning is your only reinforcement, you are likely to get frustrated and lose motivation.

### Fear, Duty, and Love

According to Kay Allan, the author of *The Journey from Fear to Love*, people use three major emotions to motivate themselves to take action. They are fear, duty, and love.

Do you want your dog to do agility because of a fear of the consequences of what you will do to her if she does not? Do you want your instructor scaring you into attempting to run clean? These are examples of the use of fear as a motivator. Do you want your dog to do agility because "she has to"? Do you practice agility because "you have to"? These are examples of duty motivation. This is not as bad as fear but still not what will help you Zone. The final motivation is love. Do you want your dog to do agility because she loves it? Do you want to compete or train because you love it?

1. **Fear.** Fear works really well as a motivator, but the problem is that you feel terrible while you are fearful. When motivated by fear, you have the short-term benefit of being extremely motivated. However, in the long run, fear motivation is very stressful and damaging. Fear is an *external* motivator. People who motivate others and dogs using fear do so because it is an ego trip. The person administering the fear feels very powerful because the response is so strong. Fear is a dangerous motivator because it burns out people and dogs. What is scientifically called *positive punishment** is a form of fear motivation.

2. **Duty.** Duty is our sense of responsibility or the "shoulds" that you impose on yourself. Duty motivation is at work when you tell yourself, "I have to do this." When you do things out of a sense of obligation, you are again *externally* motivated. I am going to go to this show because I should…, I should qualify…, or I should win… The "should" is duty.

3. **Love.** The highest and most fulfilling form of motivation is love. Love is at work in individuals who are truly passionate about their task. Love is the only motivator that is *internal.* When you love agility, you are internally motivated. When you love your dog, you are internally motivated to do what is best for her. It is possible to lure a dog around an agility course. It is possible to bribe performances. But what happens to these dogs at a competition where food is not permitted? If the dog does not *love* doing agility, she will not perform well. When trainers talk about making the obstacles reinforcing to the dog, they are talking about the process of teaching the dog to love agility. For the handler, the challenge is to make excellent handling self-reinforcing. This is usually not a problem since most competitors love the smooth and flowing runs that clear handling creates.

---

* Positive punishment is adding something like an electric shock or a leash correction to the dog's environment to reduce the likelihood of a specific behavior recurring.

Part of what you love about agility is the fun. If you do not like the word fun, then try "connection" or "flow" or whatever it is that you enjoy when you and your dog dance around an agility course. Whatever your reinforcement may be, it is causing you to be *internally* motivated to practice and succeed.

Top competitor Elicia Calhoun says "*Fun has to be first and foremost.*" By putting fun first, Elicia will easily stay motivated to practice the skills she is interested in honing.

### Making Time for Training

A common struggle for some competitors is making the time and finding a training strategy that works for them. For example, John has a new Spaniel that he is starting in agility. John already has an advanced dog in agility that does very well, but he finds that he is lacking motivation to train his young dog. John has evaluated the situation and has decided that he has several options:

1. Hire an instructor to work with him privately and give him weekly home-work assignments.

2. Keep a training journal in which he briefly jots down what he did in each training session and tracks what he would like to accomplish and by when.

3. Use the exercises in Clean Run magazine to create practice sessions or use the Clean Run Productions agility workbook series and train according to that.

John lives in a very rural area and there are few instructors available to him. In addition, these instructors live over 90 minutes away. Therefore, John has decided against option one and decided for options two and three. John also had the idea of videotaping his practice sessions so that he can then go inside and watch his own handling. This combination has helped John and his Spaniel greatly improve and become very competitive.

Dogs cannot hide what they feel. Here you can see that Loris Lewis's dog Drew is feeling anything but burned out by agility.

PHOTO BY TIEN TRAN.

### Burnout

One way to deal with burnout is to refuse to call it that. Give it a positive name like "taking a break," "reevaluating," or whatever you can think of that is *positive*.

Burnout, or needing to take a break, happens when goals have been too big, when you are externally motivated, and when you have trained too much and had too little fun. For example, Suzie is a novice competitor and chose to start competing too soon. Since Suzie and her dog are not prepared, they end up not qualifying at many shows. Suzie finds herself very frustrated and drops out of training. Later she quits agility as the result of burnout. Suzie burned out because she did not get the reinforcement that she sought. Unfortunately, Suzie decided to give up on agility rather than taking a break to give herself a fresh start. If you are having a dry spell with your dog, consider pulling your dog from competition. Continuously setting yourself up to not qualify is not fun and will lead to frustration and possibly burnout. You are also allowing your dog to rehearse unwanted behavior in the ring. If your dog consistently performs unwanted behaviors in the ring, you are training your dog to do so. Again, this can lead to handler and/or doggie burnout.

Agility instructors who are on the seminar circuit are also prone to burnout. Most of these instructors put so much into teaching that they have little left for themselves or their dogs. The lack of balance in their lives pushes them to their limit. In order to prevent burnout, instructors should take at least one day a week off and engage in non-dog activities during their free time.

So that I may be more balanced, the following are non-dog activities I am interested in:

If you are not employed full-time in dogs and still have experienced some burnout, consider a change of pace. Try taking a break from agility for a while. Start tracking, flyball, flying disc, musical freestyle, lure coursing, or some other activity that is different and new.

No matter what you decide, the cure for burnout is large doses of *fun*; fun activities for both you and the dog. Anything that is not fun is not allowed. To quote world-class competitor Pati Hatfield: "*If it is not going to be fun, why else would our dogs work so hard for us?*" When our dogs are having fun a weird thing happens—it becomes contagious.

## Leaving the Comfort Zone and Entering the Peak Performance Zone

Sometimes it is hard for people to become motivated because they have become accustomed to what they are doing. Change becomes uncomfortable. Change becomes leaving *the Comfort Zone*. People are reluctant to leave their Comfort Zone for many reasons.

Remember that the Comfort Zone may not necessarily be desirable to you, but nevertheless you feel *secure* when you stay within its comforting bounds.

An example of an agility Comfort Zone is speed. Many handlers run their dogs slowly because they feel a greater ability to control the dog. Of course, this is true; it is much easier to control a slow dog than a lightening bolt. Later, when they attempt to speed up the dog, the dog is confused. Running the dog slowly was comfortable to both the handler and the dog, thus speeding the dog up will take great effort. Zoning handlers learn to push their comfort levels. Pati Hatfield and Stuart Mah have repeatedly explained how their best runs were teetering on the edge of being out of control because of the great speed involved. Handling a bullet dog means leaving the Comfort Zone.

To leave the Comfort Zone and enter your peak performance zone, you must be motivated.

Many things can affect your motivation. What you say to yourself, the people you surround yourself with, and your view of yourself as a trainer and/or handler are all factors that impact your level of motivation.

### The Tape Recorder

The tape recorder is what you say to yourself—the words that you speak inside your head. The tape recorder can have a huge effect on your motivation. The tape recorder plays back stuff you say to yourself, but also sometimes words somebody else said. An example might be, "I am not good at handling fast dogs." This phrase gets recorded and then periodically replayed. This replaying will have a negative effect on motivation. The powerful thing to remember is that the tape recorder has an erase and re-record feature. Erase all negative statements and re-record positive ones. Then watch and wait to see what happens!

### Pleasing Others

Motivation can be affected by a desire to please. Some handlers want to do well. They like winning, but then that means they will beat other people and those other people might not be so happy. If pleasing others is your thing, you might find yourself less motivated to do your best because of a concern about other people's feelings. Sometimes someone else is reinforcing this behavior, maybe a friend or family member, and that keeps you repeating it. In order to achieve Zoning, it is a good idea to fade out the impossible desire to please everyone all the time.

### The Box

Sometimes it is difficult to find proper motivation, because you have placed yourself in a "box." The box is a label or a stereotype. For example, Joe has placed himself in the "I can't handle fast dogs" box. To Joe it seems there is no way out.

There is a way out. Joe could change his thoughts and the self-talk that he is repeating to himself ("I can't handle fast dogs."). His self-talk focuses on his limitations rather than on trying to overcome them. Limitations are *challenges*, not things he should cave in to. Joe can get out of the box by developing new ways of thinking. The "I can't handle fast dogs" becomes "I will learn to react to my very fast dog in a way that supports him." The box is gone. With the box gone, Joe now has increased motivation to train and his handling is improving.

### Impossible? The Challenge as Motivation

What have you accomplished in your past that you initially thought was impossible? Maybe the first time you took your dog to an agility class she was the only dog that hated agility. Now you see this dog doing the equipment on her own. (That is a new problem, but a better one to have.) If someone had told you this dog would love agility the first time you saw her hide under the bench to avoid being asked to take a jump, you would have said, "Impossible." Sometimes we give up too easily.

Advanced competitors may lose motivation if the stakes are not high enough. If you are concerned that this might happen to you, make sure that you raise the stakes yourself by planning to push for one of your fastest times even though you may be at a small competition. Consider having someone to report to on your run. Experiment and see what needs to happen to get you to be serious about even small competitions. Take note of what makes competition meaningful to you and duplicate it when you need to.

### If the Stakes Are Not High Enough

If the stakes are not high enough to motivate you, then you will have to raise the stakes yourself.

Competition is more meaningful to me when

```
┌──────────────────────────────────────────────────────────────┐
│                                                              │
│                                                              │
│                                                              │
└──────────────────────────────────────────────────────────────┘
```

When the stakes are not high enough my reaction has been

```
┌──────────────────────────────────────────────────────────────┐
│                                                              │
│                                                              │
│                                                              │
└──────────────────────────────────────────────────────────────┘
```

If you have found that you have lost motivation at competitions that seem less meaningful to you, how can you add meaning to these competitions?

```
┌──────────────────────────────────────────────────────────────┐
│                                                              │
│                                                              │
│                                                              │
└──────────────────────────────────────────────────────────────┘
```

### If the Stakes Are Too High

The reverse is true for less-experienced competitors. The stakes may be so high for these novice competitors that the pressure becomes too much and knocks them right out of the Zone. 99.99% of the time we set our own stakes. So if we set them too high, we can easily lower them.

I will lower my stakes by

```
┌──────────────────────────────────────────────────────────────┐
│                                                              │
│                                                              │
│                                                              │
└──────────────────────────────────────────────────────────────┘
```

In the past, when the stakes have been too high my reaction has been

In the future, I plan to prevent the stakes from getting too high by

## Success via Failure

It may seem strange that a book on success includes information on failure, but failure is what actually makes success happen. Success is the result of failure and learning. Remember your first cross-behind? Timed late and causing the dog to spin? Now you take it for granted that you can cross behind. By making mistakes, you learned how to cross behind successfully.

Failure is not a problem. When you fail to achieve the run you had envisioned, that is good. The failure opens the door to learning. Failure can lead to problems only when learning does not happen and you continue to make the same errors. Sometimes when this happens you become like a machine, repeating the same error again and again. This is the "persistent terrier syndrome." We mistakenly assume that by persisting, the outcome will eventually change. If this is what is happening, it is a good idea to try a new approach rather than repeating the same pattern.

So failure is good because it

- teaches us reality.

- teaches us to try new techniques, suggestions, and ideas.

- needs to happen in order for us to learn.

- reminds us that we are imperfect and that it is okay to be imperfect. It has been said, "show me someone who is not making mistakes and I will show you someone who is not working" or, in this case, is not handling her dog. If you are handling a dog in agility, you are going to make mistakes.

MARQ CHEEK SAYS, *"Give credit to your dog when you win and take the blame when you fail, but recognize that any error is merely another stepping stone in the learning path and you have the ability to correct for it in the future."*

When you repeatedly attempt a goal and miss it, it is important to examine whether or not your goal was realistic. It is important to check with other people who have already achieved a similar goal to see if you are on track. Do not be discouraged by what they may tell you, but carefully listen to their comments. Learn from their mistakes and adjust your goals to reality.

Marq Cheek says that it took him a couple years to get over performance jitters and a feeling that he did not want to be embarrassed. Keeping his perspective and learning from his mistakes has kept Marq and his Shetland Sheepdog Wyatt on a successful path. In 1999, Marq and Wyatt were the first handler and dog team to earn the AKC MACH title.

PHOTO BY REBECCA CHEEK.

MARQ CHEEK has the following advice for competitors who might be worried about embarrassment or something that they consider to be a failure. After all, it is the concern about failure that causes the nervousness that can negatively impact handling. Nervousness leads to fear. Fear puts our body in emergency survival mode and really confuses our dogs. Marq advises, *"You know, the jitters, butterflies, overall general nervousness. You are in a fishbowl so to speak, and you do not want to get embarrassed. It took me a couple of years to get over this one. There is virtually NOTHING that you will do that has not been done by someone else before. I have gotten lost on a course. I have knocked over a jump wing. I have tripped over a tunnel. I have fallen over my dog at a national competition and been eliminated for it. I have given a left directional when I should have yelled 'right.' In other words, do not worry about it. The ground will not swallow you up if you make a mistake. We learn from our mistakes and after all, it is just a hobby, a dog sport. There will be other days. It is a miracle we are alive. What we do for fun is insignificant in the scheme of the overall universe. I am not saying you should not care or try hard and do your best to prepare yourself and your partner, but when it comes time to run, do your best, hope for the best, and let the rest happen. Good or bad, there is always another run, another day."*

Somehow, somewhere, failure and giving up were confused as the same. You only truly fail when you stop trying, not when you miss a goal. To paraphrase Winston Churchill, *"Never, never, never… never give up."*

## 10 Motivational Tips

Sometimes a sense of failure can cause a lack of motivation. If you reach a peak in frustration regarding a training issue, it is possible to lose the motivation to practice and perhaps give up agility entirely. But even if you are not experiencing this type of frustration, the motivational tips below can be helpful.

1. **Record your training in a daily journal.** Note your reactions to training sessions and make notations for future training sessions. Place stars next to training accomplishments! Make sure to point out your accomplishments to your instructors so that they can comment on your success.

2. **Find a training partner.** Practice with someone who has similar abilities and similar goals; this will not only boost your motivation, it will also add to the fun. Inform your training partner how she can be most helpful to you and ask your training partner how you can best assist her.

3. **Find new places to practice.** Drive an hour or two to train in a strange location. A change of scenery can really change your frame of mind. Remember, if you have an inexperienced dog, start at the beginning and just reintroduce the obstacles to the dog. Do not expect the novice dog to perform as well in a new setting as she does at home. Use the time during the drive home to evaluate your training session.

4. **Attend a seminar.** Sometimes when you are in a training rut and lacking motivation, doing something simple like attending a seminar can really get you going again.

5. **Visualize a Zone run.** Visualize the run at the most exciting location you can think of. Imagine the crowd cheering you and your dog on. Apply that elated mood to all your training sessions and experience a new level of energy and enthusiasm.

6. **Relax.** There is more to life than agility training. Be sure to have some non-doggie time. Read a book, go to the movies, or participate in other activities that you enjoy. Overtraining can burn you out and extinguish motivation.

7. **Reflect on how far you have come in terms of both your handling and your training skills.** This is why it is a good idea to keep that training journal.

8. **Accept the fact that not every training session is going to go well.** All handlers and dogs have good days and bad. The challenges you encounter are always temporary. Focus on what went well.

9. **Listen to your body.** Do not ignore tired muscles or injuries. Even if they appear minor, they can distract you and result in a bad training session. In addition, minor injuries can become major ones if you ignore them. Listen to your dog. Just like you, your dog can also encounter injuries. Repeated refusals should be considered an alarm sign that an injury may be present. Ignoring your dog's signals that indicate an injury will erode your training motivation since you will become stuck experiencing the same errors.

10. **Reward yourself for training success.** Plan a relaxing getaway. Take a vacation with your dog. Go golfing, sailing, or whatever you enjoy. The idea here is to experience some balance and relaxation.

## Keeping Your Dog Motivated

While you may not have a hard time motivating yourself to practice or to sign up for trials, dogs can have motivational issues. For some dogs, agility is not reinforcing enough for them to push themselves to keep moving at top speed in 95-degree weather and no shade.

For your dog to be able to Zone with you, you will need to help her stay cool and comfortable while at the show. Playing ball with your dog for two hours prior to your run is *not* a good idea.

Just as you can be overaroused or underaroused, the same is true of your dog. Both overarousal and underarousal will cause the dog to be unable to perform at her best level.

Pay attention to the stress signals your dog might be giving you:

• Dilated pupils—can be a sign of overarousal.

• Continuous barking or whining—can be a sign of overarousal.

• Diarrhea or loose stools—while this is a sign of overarousal, it can cause underarousal because the dog may not feel well or may have low energy from not digesting food properly.

• Restlessness—depending how long the dog has been in this state, it can cause under- or overarousal.

### *Dilated pupils*

Dilated pupils can be an indicator of overarousal. Susan Garrett had to find ways to deal with a tendency toward overexcitement in her Border Collie Buzz from the first stages of training.

PHOTO BY SUSAN GARRETT.

Dilated pupils can be an indication that your dog is overaroused. Especially high-strung dogs are going to be likely to get a "wired look" in their eyes. While you might welcome this wired look as a sign that your dog is ready to perform and run like mad, it is important not to allow the wired state to continue for the whole competition. If you do allow your dog to remain wired for the entire day or weekend, it may cause the dog to totally wear out. If your dog repeatedly has "dilated pupil weekends," she may get doggie burnout.

In addition, dilated pupils can be an indication that major control issues are about to appear in the ring. Susan Garrett says that at Buzz's first show it took several attempts for her to even walk him over to the agility ring. Buzz would get overexcited when next to the ring and Susan would return him to his crate. This way Susan helped her dog understand that teamwork was up ahead, and that Buzz would not just be blasting around having fun without taking direction from Susan.

For some dogs a solution to overarousal can be to simply run them a little to get the first bursts of energy out. When they have run a little, the edge is off and they settle back down into their Zone.

Another option is to use trick training to help the dog tune into you or to gently massage the dog to calm and relax him (more information on canine massage below).

### *Continuous Barking or Whining*

Barking and whining are stressful to your dog. It would be great if this were not true and all dogs could bark their heads off, and no one would get a migraine, and the dogs would not be stressed. The reality is that barking is stressful to both canines and humans. Barking and whining are signals. When continuously barking and whining, your dog is continuously signaling. Obviously, this is going to be draining.

Teach your dog to be quiet in his crate as soon as possible. First reinforce short durations of quiet and then build up to longer and longer periods of quiet. Enlist the help of a friend so that your dog can get cookies for being quiet even when you are walking the course. Screaming at a barking dog will only increase both your stress and the stress of the dog. A Kong toy with a hole in it can be stuffed with peanut butter to keep your dog busy. This is a nice way to help your dog be correct and avoid barking.

Never take a quiet dog in a crate for granted. If your dog is great while being crated and does not cry or bark, reinforce him for that behavior. If you do not, the behavior might not be there when you really need him to be quiet.

Stress, even in practice at home, has always been an issue with Monica Percival's rescue dog, Boomer. Monica has learned that excessive licking at the start line is a key sign that Boomer will need some extra help focusing in the ring. In times of particular stress Boomer will even lick her nose while performing obstacles.

PHOTO BY TIEN TRAN.

## *Diarrhea or Loose Stools*

Diarrhea and loose stools are another stress signal. Sometimes the diarrhea is connected to barking. Alternatively, the dog might be suffering from a medical condition called stress colitis. As with all medical problems, it is always best to consult with your veterinarian. To help your dog overcome this stress reaction, make an effort to take your dog to strange places and experiment with variables to see what may be causing the stress reaction and what seems to reduce it. Consistently exposing your dog to strange places and dog shows even when you are not competing should help your dog to become desensitized to the show environment. That means that if you gradually expose her more and more, her stress reaction should become less and less.

## *Restlessness*

If your dog is continuously restless while at a show site you can help her learn to relax. Canine massage and T-Touch are great ways of doing this. Angela Wills has a Canine Massage video available for sale at (800) 796-7767. This video explains in detail how to massage your dog and help her get either relaxed or pumped up. T-Touch is very similar to Canine Massage and there are many people nationwide who demonstrate, teach, and administer T-Touch. Slow, soothing touching and speaking to your dog in a soft, calming voice will help most dogs get to a more relaxed state. Experiment and see what works best for your dog.

It all comes down to knowing your dog. If you know your dog, you will understand when she is trying to let you know that she is stressed. The next step is to experiment to find out what helps your dog relax.

Keeping your dog comfortable while she is competing is important. Of course, motivational training issues exist. This means some dogs are extremely comfortable and still not motivated to run fast. These dogs will endlessly chase a squirrel in 100-degree weather, but will wilt if asked to run in the agility ring under the same conditions. If you make it a rule to always train with speed and intensity, you will help guard against motivational issues. Teaching the dog to love agility as much as chasing a squirrel will also help maintain motivation. Motivation aside, it is still important to help your dog be comfortable. Spraying a hot dog with a water bottle is a nice thing to do. After all, she depends on you for everything. Unable to speak, she cannot ask for a cold shower. Helping your dog stay comfortable will increase your bond with your dog. That bond is what will get you those winning runs.

## Top Competitors on Training for Motivation

In agility, a motivated dog is a fast dog. Different competitors have different ideas about how to motivate a dog to run agility at light speed. Bud Houston, Pati Hatfield, and Stuart Mah all mention fun and playing games with your dog as an important step in creating the relationship that opens the door to fast agility.

BUD HOUSTON says that how you keep your dog motivated *"depends on the dog. Every dog is a riddle to be solved by his trainer. Tap into the dog's motivation and anything is possible. I think food motivation is a valuable tool for shaping performance or accuracy. But to really get a dog that works fast, playing with a sense of fun, then the dog must see agility as the game. Consider the poor animal dragging himself around an agility course, managing to go way over time. You would probably think, 'what a slow dog!' But watch the same dog out in the field five minutes later, chasing a frisbee at 7 yards per second. The dog is not slow at all! The dog's trainer has not yet bridged the connection between the two activities. The dog does not see agility as the game."*

PATI HATFIELD SAYS, *"First, handlers need to have a good understanding of how to shape a behavior and then how to reinforce that behavior to maintain its quality. Teaching/shaping the exact behavior we want is first. Often handlers will shape one parameter of the behavior (you cannot jump off the A-frame and miss the contact) but fail to shape the other parameter (nor can you creep down the A-frame at a snail's pace). If you do not know precisely what you expect, how will the dog ever know?"* Pati goes on to say, *"Once the exact performance is taught, it is necessary to motivate the dog to want to give that superior level of performance. A variable reward schedule then follows where excellent effort and performance on the dog's part is worthy of the best reward. Think of a grade of A+ needing a reward worthy of such an accomplishment, whereas a grade C performance needs a verbal 'we need to try that again.' Marking behaviors should be done during the dog's performance. If I am running a course and my dog has an excellent up dogwalk contact, you will hear me say 'yes!' to my dog the instant that first foot touches where I expect it to. Likewise, in practice, if that first footfall is not where I expect, I will stop and say, 'uh oh, what happened' and 'try again.' We will then repeat the sequence leading up to and including the dogwalk. Unacceptable performance equals having to redo your work. Excellent performance equals being made proud of the job you just did so well."*

STUART MAH RECOMMENDS, *"Begin asking for speed and quickness in practice. That way you learn to handle a faster dog in practice where you can control the situation more readily. It does not pay to have a slow dog in practice, learn to handle that way, then have a ballistic dog in the ring and have no idea of how to control him. Also, if we teach a dog to do things slowly, then he will learn that is the only way. Then when we want him to speed up on an agility course, he has no idea how. To have a fast dog in practice, the sessions need to be fun. If it feels like dreary work, then it probably is. People generally need to play more with dogs rather than just train. There has to be that special relationship between the dog and handler before you ever begin working, otherwise, you get slow methodical performances."*

When talking about training for motivation, MARQ CHEEK COMMENTED, *"All dogs and handlers become quicker and more confident in each other as they develop as a team. Team building is a multi-year effort and there are no quick and easy solutions. An eager, willing dog with an experienced handler will reach their team goal much earlier than an independent or tentative dog with an inexperienced handler."* Marq goes on to explain, *"Would you rather be 'nagged and dragged' or praised and cheered for great efforts? The answer is obvious. Having said that, avoid cheering for your dog who is performing s-l-o-w-l-y. How many times have you seen a competitor clap and carry on for a dog who is just barely getting through the weave poles even though the dog is technically perform-ing them correctly? 'Gee' says the dog, 'the slower and more accurate I am, the more dad cheers for me!' For any obstacle that is being performed slowly, the simple answer is to al-ways SIMPLIFY. If you are experiencing a slow A-frame, then lower it. If weave poles are slow, then shorten the set, widen the centerline between poles, slightly slant them, and add wires. The weave chute will allow the dog to run through the poles with speed and the wires are a non-human correction. Teach fast and you will get fast. Try to advance too quickly and you will either get a dog who makes a lot of mistakes or a dog overly con-cerned with an accurate performance; either way you have got a slow and/or inaccurate performance built in to all future competitions."*

When motivating your dog, consider the purpose for which she was bred. Usually, it will be easier to train a working or herding breed for agility than one of the independent breeds. However, almost all dogs have prey drive. If you can tap into the dog's prey drive, this can be a great source of motivation. For terriers this might be a stuffed animal on a string, which looks a little bit like a real rat that they were bred to hunt. For a sight hound, something tied to a stick that you can swing through the air might be a good start in getting the beginning of fast behavior on the agility equipment. No matter what it is that your dog is crazy about, by pairing it with agility she will learn to love the sport and be motivated to perform fast.

To achieve agility success both you and your dog must be motivated to train to the best of your abilities and keep moving toward your process goals.

Bud Houston's ability to tap into the motivation of his Sheltie, Winston, ultimately led to the duo earning their ADCH. Bud poses with judge Janet Gaunt after this accomplishment.

# Chapter 3

## *Confidence*

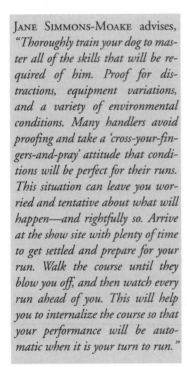

"JUST BE CONFIDENT!"

*"Be patient, give it time, pay your dues, do the best that you can, and things will come together. At the start line remember to think, 'We own this course and we own the day.'"*

—BUD HOUSTON

JANE SIMMONS-MOAKE advises, *"Thoroughly train your dog to master all of the skills that will be required of him. Proof for distractions, equipment variations, and a variety of environmental conditions. Many handlers avoid proofing and take a 'cross-your-fingers-and-pray' attitude that conditions will be perfect for their runs. This situation can leave you worried and tentative about what will happen—and rightfully so. Arrive at the show site with plenty of time to get settled and prepare for your run. Walk the course until they blow you off, and then watch every run ahead of you. This will help you to internalize the course so that your performance will be automatic when it is your turn to run."*

Have you ever run a course and everything seemed effortless? Before you ran the course and you were walking it, you remember thinking that this course, while challenging, was not a problem for you and your dog. This is what Bud Houston calls feeling like you "own this course." Part of what makes this feeling happen is confidence. When you feel confident, it is easy to get into the Zone.

Confidence is only going to happen when you and your dog have the physical skills to make a clean run happen. If you do not have the physical skills, go and practice until you are overprepared for what you will see in the ring. A good rule of thumb is to be working at least one level above the level at which you are competing. If you are competing in USDAA Starters, then you want to be training your dog at the USDAA Advanced and Masters levels. That way you will walk in the ring and feel completely overprepared for the Starters course. This will give you confidence.

Marq Cheek says the following about being confident in the competition ring, *"I think a lot of confidence comes from having a good, willing dog, attending a lot of competitions and getting the best instruction available."* Marq is introducing additional ideas that are very important for confidence: having a willing dog and getting good instruction. If your dog has medical problems, she is less likely to be willing to run agility well. Always rule out medical conditions so that you can be confident that your dog will be willing and physically able. If your dog has a medical problem, adjust your competition schedule and training schedule accordingly.

Find an instructor who helps you get the results you want. Even if this instructor is very far away, you can send videos of your training sessions and have them reviewed by the instructor.

If you find yourself overprepared and still lacking confidence, read on.

## Developing Confidence

Jane Simmons-Moake believes in thoroughly training your dog to master all of the skills required of the dog in competition, and proofing those skills in a variety of situations. Here her Golden Retriever Holly shows mastery and confidence in the poles.

PHOTO BY BILL NEWCOMB.

*"Confidence. You have to have confidence in your dog and in yourself."*

—SUSAN GARRETT

There are many techniques discussed in the following sections that will help you gain the confidence you seek.

### Be Your Own Best Friend

Next time you are running late getting to a trial or make a handling mistake, monitor the self-talk that is going through your head. Often it is something like, "You idiot! I cannot believe you are doing this again." The point is that self-talk is usually negative. Make a commitment to change that. Be your own best friend. If your best friend was late for a trial or made a handling mistake, you would not yell and insult your friend. You would be supportive and encouraging. Now treat yourself as you would your best friend. Tell yourself the same thing that you would say to your best friend. "It is okay, you are doing the best you can" or "Let me see what I can do to help you prevent that from happening in the future."

When you are kind to yourself, you are building your confidence.

### Care For Yourself

Care for yourself as you do for your dog. Get your annual checkups. Eat well. Exercise frequently. Look at yourself completely and list your different aspects—physical, spiritual, mental, and so on. Care for yourself in each of these categories. Self-care is self-respect. Self-respect is confidence. Notice special parts of yourself that you appreciate. Appreciate all aspects.

Do not expect your body to be able to withstand the stress of competing and training if you do not build up the muscles and conditioning needed. Listen to your body. If you are very sore after a weekend of competing, come up with a plan of what you might do to help your body be better prepared for the next competition. This is just as important as training your handling skills, or making sure your dog is fit enough to run.

### Be and Stay Maximally Productive

Your productivity and your confidence are completely connected. When you are maximally productive in your training, you feel very good about yourself and, as a result, your confidence soars. Training frustrations or being stuck with the same problem will block productivity. Prioritize the most important training issue, resolve that, and then move on to the next.

### *Make It a Habit to Overprepare During Warm-Up*

Competitor Mindy Lytle gives a specific example of how she uses the practice jump to be overprepared. She says it is one of her trade secrets to practice whatever she may be worried about in terms of the course at the practice jump. This helps her to be overprepared and not worry about a challenging section in the course. If she is concerned about the lead-out, she will practice that. She will attempt to duplicate the lead-out as it will be in the ring. Mindy says this has helped her keep her confidence up.

List the things you would like to teach your dog. The first thing listed is the most important and what you will start on first.

List what skills you would like to gain or improve so that you can be a better handler:

## Habit

Now make a commitment to practicing the skills that you listed above. When you commit yourself to learning something, you are committing to making the practice a habit. Habits can work either for you or against you. Competitive handlers know that the secret of great handling is a habit of continuously improving their handling abilities. Below is a poem that talks about the power of habit.

> *I am your constant companion.*
> *I am your greatest helper or your heaviest burden.*
> *I will push you onward or drag you down to failure.*
> *I am completely at your command.*
>
> *Half the things you do, you might as well turn over to me,*
> *And I will be able to do them quickly and correctly.*
> *I am easily managed; you must merely be firm with me.*
> *Show me exactly how you want something done,*
> *And after a few lessons I will do it automatically.*
>
> *I am the servant of all great men and women*
> *And, alas, of all failures as well.*
> *Those who are great, I have made great.*

*Those who are failures, I have made failures.*
*I am not a machine, though I work with all the precision of a machine*
*Plus the intelligence of a man.*

*You may run me for profit, or run me for ruin;*
*It makes no difference to me.*
*Take me, train me, be firm with me*
*And I will put the world at your feet.*
*Be easy with me, and I will destroy you.*
*Who am I?*
*I am HABIT!*

—AUTHOR UNKNOWN

When you want to make a new handling skill a habit, you have to commit to the process of habit creation. If you want your front crosses to flow and be an unconscious movement, you have to commit to practicing front crosses until they become a habit—a habit that you could do in your sleep.

## Getting Attention for Training Struggles

Sometimes it is more fun to complain about a handling skill than to commit to change it and to make the desired skill a habit. Commitment means really doing it. Commitment is not trying to do it. If you say, "I will try to learn the front cross," that is *not* commitment. *Trying* means nothing. *Doing* makes it happen.

Sometimes you become stuck in *struggle mode*. Struggle mode is when you are having a recurring training problem and talking about the problem or attempting to deal with it gets attention. This attention can be reinforcing and may actually encourage you to continue with the struggle, rather than ending it. You can end struggles by finding great instruction and then doing exactly as the instructor tells you. Consistency is very important in getting both you and the dog out of struggle mode.

To improve your handling and/or training what tasks are you committing yourself to?

```



```

## Become an Academy Award Winning Actor

In his book, *The New Toughness Training for Sports*, Dr. James Loehr talks about the competitor as an actor. The idea behind this concept is that no matter what is really happening, the competitor must act as if she were completely confident.

An Academy Award winning agility "actor" behaves in a confident way despite

- getting four hours of sleep.
- running five dogs in one competition.
- the course having the most difficult trap she has ever seen.
- having just made a handling error.

Loehr argues that movie directors do not care what is going on in the personal life of the leading lady. The director expects the actor to perform no matter what. The important thing about this acting stuff is that research shows when you behave "as if" then your brain actually begins to think it is real. Acting confident despite circumstances or needs that you may have is an acquired skill. When you watch an amazing actor perform, the performance seems real to you. This is because it is real; the actor has made it real in some way. The story the actor portrays may not be real, but the emotions are. As an agility competitor, acting confident will not only improve your performance, it will also improve the performance of your dog. Acting confident is contagious. If you are confident, your dog will feel confident too.

## Expect the Unexpected

One thing can rattle almost any competitor's confidence: the unexpected. Top competitors learn to expect the unexpected. The following are some unexpected situations and how you might remedy them.

| Unexpected | Plan |
| --- | --- |
| **Arrive late for competition.** | Smile and prepare a shortened warm-up routine. Have friends check you in. Do not set up camp, just focus on prepping your dog. |
| **Forgot important clothing or toy.** | Smile and ask yourself whether you really need this. If yes, ask to borrow it from a friend. Also, learn to warm up without it just in case. Always pack extra toys in different bags. Keep extra clothing in your truck. Be willing to help others out; you might need the favor returned sometime. |

| Unexpected | Plan |
|---|---|
| **Tiny warm-up area or no warm-up area.** | Smile and make the best of it. Have an alternative routine for you and your dog to warm up. Consider teaching your dog to jump over your outstretched arm or leg; that way you become an emergency warm-up jump. Trick training is also great for situations where you have limited warm-up space. |
| **Bad weather or other poor conditions.** | Smile and have fun anyway. Practice in the rain. Practice with rain gear on so your dog does not react to the unusual attire. Expose your dog to as many unusual settings as you can. |
| **Sudden change in running order.** | Smile and take a relaxing breath. Practice sudden changes in running order. Practice being ready to go in the ring whenever you are standing in line. Do not allow this insignificant change to control your mood or your readiness. |
| **Equipment failure, stopwatch failure, or other delay after you have prepared your dog and put her on the start line.** | Smile and take a relaxing breath. Take your dog off the start line and play with her. Practice setting up your dog in training as if you are going to start a sequence, and then don't! |

List other things you have encountered.

| Unexpected | Plan |
|---|---|
|  |  |

JANE SIMMONS-MOAKE'S advice to handlers is: *"Do not become overconfident. Convince yourself that the course will be a challenge, no matter how easy you think it may be. When you are overconfident, you may handle too loosely and cause mistakes to happen."*

If you dislike having only one plan, come up with several ideas. This will allow you to choose from several options when you actually find yourself in the unexpected situation.

Unexpected situations and being underprepared are reasons for lacking confidence. But overconfidence can also prevent you from doing your best.

Confidence is a delicate balance. Just as you cannot Zone if you are either too excited or not excited enough, you must also find the balance between being too confident and lacking enough confidence.

## Confidence and Your Dog

KATIE GREER says, *"Make sure the dogs are confident at home before setting off to trial them. Expose them to a variety of situations, crowds, and noise levels. Sometimes this is the only opportunity that a handler has to discover what may affect his dog; in that case, make a note of the happenings and work on it at home. Do not make a big deal of it at the trial. Much of the time what may affect a dog one day does not the next. Too often I see dogs who really could have benefited from more training on an individual obstacle before venturing out to add it to a moving sequence. Running full out at an obstacle during the excitement of a trial is quite different from performing it alone in the backyard."*

For your dog to run courses confidently, she must be exposed to a variety of equipment in training. Not all teeters tip at the same point. Some dogwalks are rock solid while others vibrate as your dog gallops up and across. Not all weave poles look the same. So again, exposing your dog to different equipment in different environments is of crucial importance. Without this prior experience, a dog's performance may lack confidence.

A course with many tight turns can slow down an otherwise confident dog if she has not been trained to perform fast, tight turns away from home. Dogs do not generalize what they have learned very well. This means that just because "Speedy" learned to turn tight and fast at home does not mean she will know how to do this at a match or at a competition. Taking your dog to different locations to practice will help Speedy generalize and understand that tight turns are always fast.

Agility can cause you, as a trainer, to have a preoccupation with the obstacles. What actually makes for beautiful and smooth-flowing agility is what happens *between* the obstacles. Pati Hatfield heavily emphasizes the importance of handling the dog's path and not the obstacles. The same applies to training: practice and learn to handle the dog's path and your dog will be more confident executing the obstacles.

Because some dogs are highly intuitive in their learning style, sometimes we outright forget to train certain behaviors. Intuitive dogs are very good at guessing what we mean. The problem begins when the dogs start guessing wrong. So if your dog learned something super fast, be suspicious about whether she actually did absorb the information or whether she was just guessing really well. Proofing the behavior and making sure it has generalized will help prevent your dog from guessing and maybe guessing wrong.

Katie Greer exposed her Chihuahua Samson to a variety of situations before taking him to his first trial. This gave him plenty of confidence when making the transition from the backyard to competition ring.

PHOTO BY TIEN TRAN.

KATIE GREER suggests that you help your dogs to *"be correct when they are not sure. Make things easier, lower jumps, and reward good effort. As the dogs become more confident, then up the ante on them. Never be afraid to back up and show them what it was that you wanted. To leave a dog guessing simply is not fair to him at all and eats at his confidence. If this shows up unexpectedly at a trial, then be prepared to take the NQ and do what it is that will benefit the dog in the long run. There is always another trial. Introduce the strange and unusual to dogs during practice so that they will come to expect the unexpected. It should all be a game and the dogs should be thinking that this is a new trick the handler has devised for them that they need to outsmart us on."*

What Katie is talking about is proofing. Proof behaviors by testing if the dog still performs the behavior even in the absence of a reward. Next, continue proofing by testing if the dog does the behavior under distraction. Finally, build up to working her under the massive distraction of food, toys, lots of noise, and other dogs. Jane Simmons-Moake has an excellent videotape series that has great ideas for proofing (available through Clean Run Productions at 1-800-311-6503).

Pati Hatifield reminds us that it is the handler's job to make sure the dog is comfortable learning and to build confidence in the dog. Here is Pati with her very confident Malinois Lilly.

<small>PHOTO BY PAM HATFIELD.</small>

PATI HATFIELD works hard to set up her dogs for success and to help her students accomplish the same. Pati says, *"A dog's confidence is built on how we train. Regardless of whether the dog is soft or sensitive by nature, it is the handler's responsibility to create a working relationship where the dog is comfortable learning. Put yourself in the dog's shoes. Imagine you have a new job and although excited about the new position, you are somewhat nervous about learning the new tasks and responsibilities. Now what kind of boss/coach would you want? One who emphasizes your mistakes or one who gently points out your errors, but primarily focuses on what you did right? A good working relationship means that the dog will be sensitive to his handler's emotions. Are we feeling confident on course or are we nervous or worried about qualifying? How can we expect one thing from our dogs, but something different from ourselves?"*

When proofing, it is very important that you do not make every repetition harder than the previous one. This means that it is best to *ping-pong* the dog. For example, the dog is practicing the weave poles. For one repetition the dog is subjected to the distraction of tennis balls lying on the ground while she weaves. The next repetition there might only be *one* ball lying farther away. This means that during the second repetition the distraction actually got easier. In the next repetition, the distraction gets harder again. Every once in a while go back to doing the poles with no distraction at all. This ping-pong effect of one repetition harder, and one easier, enables the dog to be less aware of your raising your standards. Ping-ponging is especially important for the independent breeds such as terriers or Beagles.

As with all training, you want to end a proofing session on a positive note; you can do this by ending on a particularly successful repetition and giving your dog a *jackpot*. A jackpot is when you give your dog a handful of treats at one time. Remember to always reward stellar performances with extra special rewards.

It is best to prevent any errors during the proofing process. If your dog actually gets distracted and pops out of the weave poles, you have done too much. Every time you get an error in training, you are actually practicing that error. Setting up your dog for success is very important to avoid patterning mistakes.

It is your job to help the dog feel confident. It is unfair to expect the dog to somehow give you the confidence you need to successfully complete your run. When you build your confidence, the dog's confidence will grow as a result.

Dogs essentially require four things from us to be confident:
• They need us to teach them what they need to know.
• They need us to signal clearly.
• They need us to proof them.
• They need us to make it fun.

## Confidence and Challenging Sequences and Courses

You can build your confidence by practicing challenging sequences and courses. Keep a notebook of all the courses you have run. Jot down simple notes about what was a particular challenge to you. Even if you did not run the course but watched a majority of handlers struggle with a specific course segment, jot down the segment and start practicing.

Remember to set up yourself and your dog for success. Do this by softening hard angles and increasing the space between obstacles. Do whatever you need to, so that you and your dog complete the sequence successfully. Once you are consistently able to do so, it is time to tweak the segment and increase the difficulty.

### *Example*

Paul and his dog Tiger are having a hard time when a judge places a spread jump before the weave poles. Somehow, Tiger always overshoots the weave pole entrance and earns a refusal.

Paul sets up the sequences below. His plan is to begin with Figure 1 on the first day. He will proceed to Figure 2 on the second day, and so on, until he has completed his triple to weave pole training.

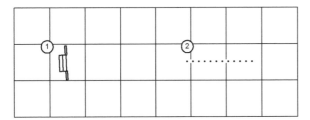

**Figure 1** In this sequence, Paul allows plenty of space between the triple and the weaves. This gives Paul lots of room to avoid the refusal. He does not want to rehearse any mistakes. The first time he works this sequence he leads out. He then gradually decreases the distance of his lead-out until he is able to run the sequence with his dog on either side.

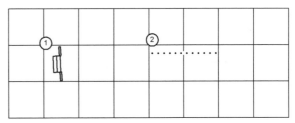

**Figure 2** Paul has now made the sequence harder by moving the poles closer to the triple. Again, he begins with leading out to be able to micromanage the entry and prevent the refusal. Again, he slowly eliminates the lead-out and works his dog on both sides.

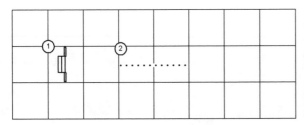

**Figure 3** The triple is now at minimum distance (15 feet) from the weave poles. Paul realizes that it is very unlikely to see the triple set this close to the weaves in competition, but he is building confidence by training this way. If he can train to hit this entry, he can definitely hit it when a judge gives him more room. Again, he slowly eliminates the lead-out and works his dog on both sides.

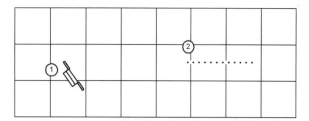

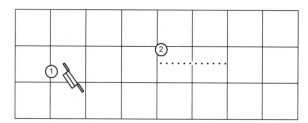

**Figure 4** Now Paul is experimenting with angles. Notice that the triple is pulled far from the weave poles, just like it was in Figure 1. Paul is doing this to make it easy for Tiger and him. Paul will be changing the angle of the triple while he maintains the same distance, so that he may be prepared and confident regardless of what angle is presented at a competition. Again, he slowly eliminates the lead-out and works his dog on both sides.

**Figure 5** Paul has moved the poles closer. Again, Paul will be playing with the angle of the triple so that Tiger is prepared for all possible angles. Again, he slowly eliminates the lead-out and works his dog on both sides.

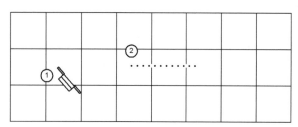

**Figure 6** In this final exercise, Paul is combining the tight distance with a harsh angle. Again, he slowly eliminates the lead-out and works his dog on both sides. Paul is now very prepared for a triple to the weaves combination. His confidence is soaring. Interestingly, Paul notices that both his handling and his dog's performance have improved from this training.

Take a moment to think about what your three most common errors are, and write them below:

Now jot down the sequences that have caused these errors to occur. Using Paul's system, develop your own training plan for training your dog to accurately perform the sequences that have been a challenge to you.

## *Example*

Brenda has the same problem as Paul. Her dog Belle also has trouble when approaching the weave poles at a great speed. After careful analysis of the situation, Brenda decides that the chute is the most difficult obstacle for Belle to enter the weaves from. Brenda has compiled a list of the easiest to the hardest obstacles before the weaves for her and the dog. Her list looks like this:

### Easiest to Hardest

Teeter to the weaves

Dogwalk to the weaves

A-frame to the weaves

A regular jump to the weaves

A winged jump to the weaves

A spread jump to the weaves

A winged spread jump to the weaves

Tunnel to the weaves

Chute to the weaves

When Brenda begins practicing, she varies which obstacle she places in front of the weaves; but she is careful not to place the more difficult ones in front of the weaves. Like Paul, Brenda plays with the angles and distance in front of the poles to set Belle up for success. When Brenda does this, she is careful to always start with something easy and then slowly move on to the harder spacing or angle.

During this process she periodically goes back to very simple exercises, allowing Belle and her the easy success of a very simple approach to the poles. Brenda is careful to jackpot her dog for extremely great performances.

Finally, Brenda has worked her way to the chute. After a few weeks of training every day, she is now managing to hit the weave pole entrance from any angle with her dog coming out of the chute. Belle can now hit her entry, after coming out of the chute, even with distractions.

However, Brenda has a new problem now. Belle liked these exercises so much that now she has weave pole "suck." Given the choice Belle will suck into the weaves quite easily. Brenda laughs about this and within a few days she has Belle performing the poles only when she gives the command. Brenda did this by showing Belle that she is only going to get a reward when Brenda *asks* her to do the weave poles.

## Questions to Ask Yourself

| | |
|---|---|
| 1. In the past, what has helped you feel confident? | |
| 2. What worked to get your confidence up when you were experiencing a lack of confidence? | |
| 3. In the future, how are you going to ensure that you feel confident at every competition? | |

## Chapter 4

# Thought Power

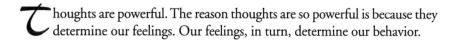

*Watch your thoughts; they become words.*
*Watch your words; they become actions.*
*Watch your actions; they become habits.*
*Watch your habits; they become character.*
*Watch your character; for it becomes your destiny.*

—Author unknown

Thoughts are powerful. The reason thoughts are so powerful is because they determine our feelings. Our feelings, in turn, determine our behavior.

Thought → Feeling → Behavior

Apply this to agility. If a handler thinks, "My handling is terrible," she will feel less confident as a result. If this handler then proceeds to run her dog, she is likely to encounter problems during her performance.

If you want to enter your agility achievement Zone, you have to check your negative thoughts at the door.

## How the Unspoken Impacts Performance

Psychologists say that 80% of what we communicate is *unspoken*. People communicate their thoughts and feelings in their body language, at times even without intending to do so. It is the unspoken which influences the decisions you make while communicating with other people. Our dogs do the same. It is the unspoken that our dogs listen to.

Dogs do not have ESP (Extra Sensory Perception). Dogs read our thoughts through our behavior. Dogs are the Einsteins of reading body language. Let's examine how this works. You think, "She is going to miss the weave pole entrance!" Immediately your muscles begin to tighten. You clench your jaw and make a stress face. The dog sees this, and reads that this is *not* how mom usually looks. Now the dog is distracted and is also getting tense. The dog sees the first weave pole, but it is too late. She has missed the entrance.

If you question whether this is true, consider the story of Clever Hans. Clever Hans was a horse that was able to solve simple math problems. Many people would observe Hans while he would be solving simple math problems and all stated that the owner gave no cues to the horse. Any person in the room could ask Hans something like "What is 3+6?" and Hans would tap out the answer using his front hoof. Even some psychologists were fooled into actually believing that Hans could understand and solve math problems. Finally, someone came up with the idea of testing Hans's math abilities without his owner being present. Sure enough, Hans could not answer any questions if his owner was not there. Closer observation showed that the owner was accidentally giving Hans very subtle cues. For example, the owner would hold his breath while Hans was counting and would exhale when Hans reached the correct number. The owner was also cueing Hans with his facial expressions. While Hans was counting, he would tense his brow, and when Hans reached the proper number, he would relax. Clever Hans's story demonstrates how acutely aware animals are of our facial expressions and our breathing.

Dogs cue off your body both intentionally when you signal, and unintentionally when you do not intend to signal them. The problems begin with the latter. That is why many handlers encounter problems only in competition. These dogs become "ring wise" because of the accidental cues of their handlers.

Back to the example of the dog that missed the weave pole entrance because her owner accidentally distracted her with unfamiliar cues of clenching her jaw muscles and tensing her body. This handler has two ways to break out of the cycle. First, she can practice thinking that missing the weave pole entrance is not a big deal. She can take the pressure off by saying, "If we miss the entrance, we will still have a good time." The handler could also tell herself, "If we miss the entrance, my dog will only have done what I told her to do." This thought will guard against frustration building up. Second, the owner can become aware of her reactions and her facial expressions. If she feels herself tensing up as she approaches a tricky part of the course, she can breathe deeply and relax. The handler could apply her *negative-thought prevention roll-on*. This roll-on, similar to a deodorant, will guard against any negative thoughts. The roll-on method is a fun and figurative way of preventing negative thoughts from entering her mind.

Pati Hatfield's Malinois Lilly experiencing absolutely no problem with the weave poles.

PHOTO BY TIEN TRAN.

Ken Boyd runs his dog for all-out fun. Negative thoughts have nowhere to latch on because he is gung-ho on having a blast. Ken lets his dog see that he is having fun and that makes the dog have fun. This "positive vicious cycle" has worked extremely well for Ken and his dog Becky, who won the Triple Crown of dog agility (the AKC, NADAC, and USDAA Nationals) in 1997. Ken recommends not even allowing thoughts of *"playing it safe."* He says that when he was preparing to run Becky at all three of the national finals he kept telling himself, *"No matter what, I am not going to play it safe."* He made the decision that they were going to go all out. *"All or nothing"* is how they practiced and "all or nothing" is how they ran.

When Ken competes, he thinks about *"fun and going for it."* Clearly, his dog Becky is able to read these thoughts in his expressions and body language.

An integral part of what makes Ken and Becky a winning team is the positive thoughts that Ken chooses to think.

### What Is in a Name?

Have you noticed the names of a lot of the top competition dogs and how they create mental images? Spiffy, Nifty, Awesome, Lazer, Riot, Buzz, Twister, Time Flies, Flurry, Danger, Turbo, Nitro, and Flash—all of these names conjure up images of speed. It is not necessary that you name your dog something that sounds fast, but it is helpful to give the dog a name that creates a positive mental image for you. After all, what we name our dogs is going to significantly impact our thoughts, feelings, and ultimately our behavior toward those dogs.

Susan Garrett explains that she feels that the dog's nickname is even more relevant than the dog's name. Susan mentioned that she once met a man who nicknamed his dog "Idiot." He would say it in a playful kind of way; however, he had many training problems with his dog. Agility success is dependent on your relationship with your dog. If you name your dog Idiot, it will not have a positive effect on your relationship.

Nicknames aside for a moment, let us pretend someone has named her dog "Napoleon." Is it hard to imagine that this dog might develop a strong personality and that the owner might then begin thinking of him as very stubborn and difficult to handle?

One handler named his five-pound dog "Spike" and had chronic training problems with him. Because Spike was so tiny the handler was not bothered by Spike growling at him; actually he thought it was really cute. And it went well with the name. He also did not mind too much that Spike used his house as a toilet. Needless to say, Spike required a lot of work in his training, both on and off the agility field.

To what extent is your dog's name impacting your thoughts about your dog and ultimately your interaction with the dog? Only you can say for sure. Thinking of your dog as resistant and obstinate is not going to be helpful to the training process. Ultimately your thoughts create your attitude toward your dog and your attitude determines your success as an agility team.

Jean Donaldson, author of *Culture Clash*, says that dogs are amoral and pretty much *"black input/output boxes."* She goes on to say that because of this fact we condition them to behave as they do. Ultimately, you can create your dog's personality. So, you name the young puppy Napoleon, and then complain about his behaving like Napoleon. The dog is now getting attention for obnoxious and persistent behavior, and thereby reinforced for the Napoleonic behavior. It does not take long (insert the sound of loud trumpets, Ta! Da!) and you have a Napoleon!

The truth is that *we* do select certain behaviors and reinforce them in the dog. This is what ultimately creates the dog's personality. Even irritating characteristics are reinforced if they are given attention, whether negative or positive attention. So our thoughts about our dogs and how we view their personality are little things that make a big difference. Try changing your thoughts about Napoleon's personality and see if his behavior changes. If you stop thinking that he is difficult and start focusing on reinforcing the times when he is not being difficult, Napoleon may be purring in your hands like a kitten.

## Attitude and Training

JULIE DANIELS gives an example of how even when your general attitude toward your dog is ideal, you can run into trouble if you allow negative thoughts to creep in during competition. Julie describes how she uses thought power: *"If I did not like the course on initial walk-through (for example, perhaps the opening sequence is too harsh and de-motivating for sensitive Arrow), I have to change my attitude. There will be no Zone run if I cannot get past this argument with the course. I cannot afford to be thinking, 'This is fine for Spring, but Arrow will shut down if I call him off three things in a row so soon.' I have to turn that around quickly, perhaps, 'I will back cross twice at the first two obstacles, then front cross here, and Arrow will like the opening.' That is where my focus has to be. We have turned in many clean runs with unfriendly openings, closings, or anything else, but a Zone run will not happen unless I am at peace with the course for that dog. Sometimes I have to be Dr. Jekyll with one dog and Mr. Hyde with another. To Zone, I have to be completely who that dog needs, not somewhere in the middle. The Zone is always elusive if I am not 100% tuned in to that individual dog."*

Different dogs are going to have different levels of sensitivity to your thoughts and feelings. Julie Daniels refers to this by saying that she needs to be a totally different handler from one dog to the next.

Try videotaping two runs. During the first run, make a stern face and do not allow the dog to see that you are having fun. No matter how much fun you are actually having, refuse to smile or look happy. The more fun you have, the sterner and tighter your face should get. Make sure to think that your dog will miss the weave pole entrance. Become obsessed with this thought. Begin thinking about it before the run even starts, and as you approach the poles make yourself tense up as much as possible.

Then run your dog again. This time, smile and be ecstatic the whole time. No matter what the dog does you are happy. If the dog takes five off-course obstacles, smile and be happy. Dance around. During this run you allow *no* negative thoughts. For the second run, make sure that you run a different course pattern at the same level as the first run. This will guard against the dog anticipating the obstacles.

Now watch the video to see how your dog responds to your expressions and body language. Make notes about the changes that you saw in your dog. Which dog would you rather have in the show ring? Dog A, which was your dog and how she responded to the first "refusing to have fun" run, or dog B, which was the "have fun no matter what" run. Which dog would be more fun to run? Which dog would be more likely to consistently do well in the ring?

You can continue to experiment until you find what expressions are most effective for your dog. Also experiment with the tone of your voice and the volume that you use. Some dogs love loud cheering; others can be distracted by it. Please note that you never want to cheer your dog when she is performing poorly. Cheering a slow dog or one that is making mistakes simply reinforces what you do not want. If a dog slows and you cheer the dog, she will sometimes temporarily speed up. This rewards you for the cheering. However, in the long run the dog will slow again. Cheer only if the dog likes it, and only when the dog is knocking your socks off.

No matter what handling style your dog prefers, you will need to smile. Smiling lets the dog know that you are having fun. In an ideal situation, you successfully block all nervous thoughts. Sometimes competitors are not able to eliminate all nervous thoughts. If this happens, do not allow your body to mirror the nervous thoughts. A dog cannot get a reading on your nervousness if your body is relaxed and smiling.

Julie Daniels explains the importance of being *"at peace"* with the course for the particular dog she is running in order to Zone. Her very enthusiastic Border Collie Spring is much different to run than her sensitive English Springer Spaniel Arrow.

PHOTOS BY TIEN TRAN AND KATHY PEPIN, RESPECTIVELY.

### Free Instruction from Your Anxious Thoughts

Jill is warming up and it all feels wrong. Her dog is messing up and she is feeling tense and anxious. Now what? Jill decides not to give her anxiety any power. Instead, Jill begins gathering important information from her anxiety. What is the anxiety trying to tell her? Is the anxiety saying, "We did not train enough to be running this course?" Or is the anxiety there because this course requires some very tight turns that Jill's dog is not prepared for? When you get a flood of anxiety, it is very important to understand what the anxiety is about. This way you can get free instruction from your anxiety. It may be too late to implement this information if you are already at a show, but you can certainly use what you learned before the next competition.

## Positive Thoughts No Matter What

In the ideal situation, you do not have anxious thoughts creeping in at the last minute. In this situation, you can think positively no matter what. Thinking positively in competition requires the same process that you use to teach your dogs. Use the *shaping process* that is used to train dogs to train yourself to think positively. Begin with acknowledging any positive thoughts that you are having. Next, move to changing negative thoughts into positive ones. Then, finally, reward yourself for longer and longer periods of not having a negative thought. Do not scold yourself for having negative thoughts. Remember that the negative thought could be giving you valuable information.

You may want to use some of Karen Pryor's *Laws of Shaping* to help you accomplish this task:

- Raise criteria in increments small enough so that you always have a realistic chance at reinforcement.

- Train only one thing at a time. Do not try to work on preventing negative thoughts and a handling move at the same time.

• If you are having a bad day, lower your criteria and "go back to kindergarten." You can then raise criteria more rapidly than before when you try again another day.

Ultimately, thinking positively will be its own reward.

## Winning and Qualifying

Bud Houston says *"Your thoughts need to center around your objective: to create a positive environment and experience for the dog."* The human thoughts about winning and agility fame are *"counterproductive to the dog."* It takes mental discipline to work on this, but competitive thinking does not work for the dog. Your job as the handler is to make each run a positive experience for the dog.

Guess what? Your goal in agility cannot be to qualify or win. If your thoughts focus on winning or qualifying, you are increasing your chances for disqualifying yourself. This is true for various reasons. First, thinking about winning before you actually run your dog can cause pressure. Pressure can bump you right out of the Zone. Also, thoughts of winning can cause you to be overconfident and, again, you are booted right out of the Zone. Because agility is a team sport, thoughts and the resulting pressure or overconfidence also affects your dog negatively.

Handlers who consistently succeed in the competition ring are those who think about what it is that their dog needs from them. By centering their thoughts on how they might best support their dog they, more often than not, become the handlers to qualify and win.

Susan Garrett and her Border Collie Stoni have proved time and time again that nothing is impossible. Stoni has won two USDAA national championships, and is the only dog to have won all three of the USDAA national tournaments: Dog Agility Masters (DAM), Steeplechase, and Grand Prix of Dog Agility.

PHOTO BY LYNN SICKINGER.

## Thoughts at the Start Line

Frequently we are bombarded with useless or non-helpful thoughts when we step up to the start line. Elicia Calhoun says that one of the thoughts that can interfere with her run is when she gets overly concerned with a certain obstacle or segment. Elicia says that when this happens she has a hard time enjoying the run. The solution she recommends is just not giving into the temptation of allowing yourself to become overly concerned with anything in the course you are about to run.

One technique that is useful in ending unwanted thoughts is called *thought-stopping*. To use this technique, simply tell yourself *"Stop!"* when you begin having an undesirable thought. Like all the mental handling skills, this technique takes time to develop. Begin practicing using thought-stopping in training. First, catch yourself thinking a negative thought. This part alone takes some time to develop. Frequently we think negative thoughts so often that we do not even notice. Second, implement thought-stopping by saying *"Stop!"* either silently or aloud. Make sure to acknowledge your success. Be aware that initially you will need to use this technique repeatedly. You will succeed in stopping a thought and a few minutes later catch yourself having it again. Be patient and consistent. More information on thought-stopping and similar techniques is included in the book *Feeling Good* by David Burns.

Elicia Calhoun tries hard to avoid getting overly concerned with a certain obstacle or segment on course as she says it interferes with her run. Here, Elicia guides her Australian Shepherd Suni through the course.

PHOTO BY ARDIS LUKENS.

So you have succeeded at ridding yourself of all negative thoughts, now the task at hand is to make the start line the most fun place to be for you and your dog.

Make a game out of getting ready at the start line by telling your dog "Ready, steady, go!" or any other phrase that is energizing and fun to you. "Ready" (deep inhale, think, "This is going to be a blast"), "Steady" (deep exhale, think "We are now entering the Zone"), "Go!"

Some handlers like to play games with their dogs at the start line that let them know when the dogs are ready. Several top handlers use the technique of waiting for a certain look, or a little whine, or bark from their dogs before they go. Only you can know what game will work best for you and your dog. Experiment to find the right game for you. Consider coming up with a couple of start line games so that you can alternate.

## Become the Dog

You can use thought power in competition, but it is also necessary and very useful in training. Let us say that you have been training your dog on weave poles and she is actually getting worse. The more you work with the dog, the worse the poles get. First, she was popping out at the tenth pole. Now it is at the eighth pole, and sometimes she is coming out even earlier. You are about to explode. Why is this happening? After all, the dog has been weaving for years.

Now is the time to try out the technique of *becoming the dog*. First, try to do this when the frustration is actually occurring. Say you were training your dog, and she just popped out of the weave poles. You are feeling like either pulling your hair out or quitting agility altogether. Quick, grab a notepad and begin writing. Write down how you feel first and purge.

Next, step into the shoes—oops, paws—of your dog and see what she sees. What does your dog want to say to you? What is she thinking? Write down everything that comes to mind while "you have become your dog." This is very valuable information.

This is the order of events so far:

1.  Frustrating training problem occurs.
2.  You write down *your* reaction and feelings about what happened.
3.  You write down what the dog might say if she could speak.
4.  You use the information to revamp training program.

In step three, you are actually writing down what you think your dog would tell you if she could talk. This is the ultimate humanization—of course, dogs do not actually think what you will be writing. This exercise is about what *you* are projecting. A *projection* is attributing your thoughts to someone else or to your dog. When you write down what your dog would tell you if she could, you are really writing down your projection. This is important to do because it gets the information out in the open. You are then free to do something with it, if you choose.

### Example

Ann has decided to use this technique to develop new training ideas. First, some background information on Ann. She is 45 years old and is happily married with no kids. Currently Ann is very unhappy in her job. She frequently feels ignored by her boss when she asks him for important information that she needs to do her job. Her dog Bullet is a very fast Beagle. Bullet is a six-year-old, neutered male. Bullet has been very successful in agility, but Ann has encountered consistency problems with him.

One day Ann goes to work and her boss is worse than ever. Ann ends up spending the entire day attempting to get the information that the boss requested and does not succeed. She goes home that night frustrated, because she feels that she was unable to accomplish anything. That evening Ann goes to agility class. She was looking forward to the fun of running her dog, but soon Bullet is sniffing the ground and totally distracted by rabbit dung. Ann reaches a peak frustration level. She grabs her notepad and begins writing.

Ann's reaction to her frustrating training session: *I am totally frustrated with Bullet right now. Bullet is not running well tonight and I am not having fun. I am so completely frustrated by my dog I am ready to quit agility. I think I must be insane to be spending money on classes when my dog has no interest in this sport. It is obvious to me that you are totally ignoring me. You are doing this on purpose because you want me to stop torturing you with this agility training. It is obvious that I do not matter to you. You are an ungrateful dog, even after all of the things I have done for you. I spend so much time with you. I do not have a social life, so you can have fun and the thanks is that you ignore me.*

Notice how Ann assumes that Bullet is ignoring her. This perception is really coming from the frustrating situation at work. Furthermore, Ann feels that Bullet is ungrateful and doing the sniffing deliberately just to upset her. This is also not accurate, but it seems that way to Ann.

What Ann thinks Bullet would say to her if he could talk: *When you came home from work, you already had your face all scrunched up. You looked all stressed and like you had a bad day. I kept thinking I must have done something bad and was avoiding you. You did not notice this. When we got to class today, you did not smile or at anytime look like you were having any fun. That really stresses me.* **You are so inconsistent.** *Sometimes coming here is a blast and other times you are all distracted and seem far away. You also did not focus on me. I got more stressed and had to sniff around and then I found these yummy rabbit poopies. Then you got mad and I did not want to play anymore. If this is how agility is going to be, I do not want to play.*

In this statement, Ann learns that Bullet is not having fun but is stressing, and that "ignoring" has nothing to do with the problem. She also realized that Bullet gets distracted when she gets distracted. Like Susan Garrett says, *"our dogs are simply a reflection of us."* Ann is now clear about what she must do. Ann has made a decision either not to go to class when she has had a bad day or learn to leave the bad day at work and have fun with her dog. In addition, Ann is going to be aware of her own focus and attention. She sees a connection now between Bullet's distraction and her own distraction, and how Bullet's inconsistency is really the result of her own inconsistent behavior.

Ann was able to become clear about what was really going on and what needs to happen in her training sessions by using the *become-the-dog technique*. Ann has obviously gained very valuable information from this exercise.

Take a moment now to think about the most frustrating training situation you have ever had. Describe the situation and your reaction and feelings about the training problem below.

```
┌─────────────────────────────────────────────────────────┐
│                                                         │
│                                                         │
│                                                         │
│                                                         │
└─────────────────────────────────────────────────────────┘
```

Now, if you became your dog, what would you say to your handler about the frustrating training situation above? Include what you think the dog thinks about you as well as about the actual obstacle or obstacle sequence.

```
┌─────────────────────────────────────────────────────────┐
│                                                         │
│                                                         │
│                                                         │
│                                                         │
└─────────────────────────────────────────────────────────┘
```

Now write down ideas for how you can CHANGE your training style to prevent your frustration from recurring.

```
┌─────────────────────────────────────────────────────────┐
│                                                         │
│                                                         │
│                                                         │
│                                                         │
└─────────────────────────────────────────────────────────┘
```

PATI HATFIELD says that when her students leave the ring, no matter what type of run they had, *"They better be able to tell me what they did well."* Pati wants them to *"focus on the good things."* She further recommends, *"No sulking, or if you have to sulk, give yourself a time period (two minutes to one hour) to sulk."* Then she recommends *"letting it go."*

### *Praise and Positive Reinforcement*

Agility training should use rewards of fun, food, and praise. The agility training area is a positive and fun area. The same rule of focusing on the positive and praising is true for us. If you send your dog into the wrong end of the tunnel and get frustrated, try praising yourself for noticing that your shoulders were pointing toward the opposite entrance than you intended. It is always possible to find a positive. Sometimes it is just a little more challenging. Celebrate your handling accomplishments. Remember back a few years ago and give yourself credit for the huge improvement in handling you have made.

## Reaction versus Proaction

Okay, here are the facts: when you react rather than proact, you are giving away the only control that you have. Say you have a run that is less than what you wanted. You are mad. You are mad at the dog and you pick her up and put her in her crate to "think about it." You just reacted. You did not *proact*. You reacted to your frustration about the situation. When proacting, you do not blame the dog. For example, if your young dog is losing focus in competition after a few obstacles, you can react and blame the dog, saying that she is stupid or never pays attention. Or, you can proact and say that the dog is inexperienced and needs more training. When you react and say that the dog is deliberately taking the off-course tunnel just to spite you, you have lost control to alter the situation. Attributing a wrong course to a dog deliberately misbehaving is humanization. But, if the dog did deliberately misbehave and did not do what she has been trained to do, whose fault is that? No matter how you look at it, the dog's behavior in the agility ring is *always* a training issue.

Next time you get ready to react to a situation take a deep breath and proact. Evaluate your part in the problem and work on that, since that is what you can control.

### *Hot Buttons*

In his book, *The Achievement Zone*, Dr. Shane Murphy talks extensively about *hot buttons*. A hot button, when pressed, ignites us emotionally. Dogs know our hot buttons and sometimes press them just for the reaction. Mind you, to the dog, any reaction can be reinforcing. So even if you are leaping and cursing, this can be amusing to the dog and reinforcing to her.

The law of the hot button goes like this: the more stressed you are the larger your button grows, and the larger the eruption when your hot button is pressed. This seems tremendously unfair, since when we are stressed we would like the hot button to be tiny so that no one can find it. Instead of the hot button cutting us some slack, it gets huge and really cranks up the reaction knob. Understanding this dynamic is half the battle.

Learn to identify what triggers your hot buttons and when.

List the triggers below.

```



```

In what situations is your hot button especially huge and prone to massive eruption?

```



```

What are your feelings and thoughts when your hot button is pressed?

```



```

What happened before your hot button was pressed? What were the events that led up to it? These situations are triggers and it is important to be able to anticipate them.

```



```

In the past, what has helped you to be proactive rather than reacting when your hot button is pressed?

```



```

What have friends and family members suggested with regard to your hot button?

```



```

When your hot button gets pressed in competition, what has been helpful and what was not helpful?

```



```

What is your plan of *action* for the next time your hot button is pressed?

When you have been able to distract yourself from reacting to your hot button, how did you do that?

If your hot button is pressed, practice the following steps:

1. Take a deep breath and count to 4,872. Okay, seriously, count for as long as you have to. The idea is to be aware of your breathing and to use it to calm yourself. You do not need to resist feeling the eruption, but it is important not to react to it. Just let your emotions happen, but do not yell or scream or kick. You are not holding it in, you are just letting it pass. Just like getting your blood drawn, it is uncomfortable but does not require you to run screaming from the room.

2. Focus on something positive and absorbing. Distract yourself. Go play tug with your dog or run around the field for a few minutes. Emotional reactions create a hormonal reaction inside of us. By moving around you are metabolizing those hormones more quickly than you would just sitting still. Use the energy that the eruption has given you in a positive and constructive way, such as

   • playing fetch with your dog and throwing the toy as hard as you can.

   • going for a run around the field with your dog.

   • going for a quick jog with a friend.

   • playing frisbee with your dog.

   • doing anything that keeps you moving and helps you burn off that energy that has been kicked up by your hot button being pressed.

### Example

You have been working with your dog on avoiding tunnel traps. You have had several frustrating runs in which the dog sucked into the tunnel on an otherwise clean run. You have developed a habit of worrying about the tunnels on a course. You make it to the regional USDAA Grand Prix qualifier and

Become a handling champion—don't let your dog push your hot button on course.

your dog sucks into the tunnel. Your hot button is pressed. The volcano is now glowing with lava. Instead of exploding, you take a deep breath, exhale, finish your course, and start running around the ring cheering and praising your dog. The spectators think you are a raging maniac, but you have done a great thing.

You have

- broken the pattern of "freaking out" over the tunnel suck. It is always good to break a negative pattern.

- immediately replaced the negative frustrating thought you were having with a positive, fun thought.

- replaced your reactive behavior with constructive proactive behavior.

- evened out the emotional up and down of competition by stubbornly refusing to allow anything that happens in the ring to keep you from having a good time.

Please remember that not reacting to your hot button is a Masters level skill. When we successfully accomplish this, we are *handling champions.* Be patient with yourself. This is no easy feat. The course times are extremely tight and it takes a great deal of practice to successfully maneuver an avoiding-the-hot-button course.

### Feelings

Feelings evoke reactions. Fear is the feeling that evokes the strongest reactions. Competitors develop fears around being embarrassed or certain situations like being the first dog in the ring.

Mindy Lytle recommends that if you have a fear of being the first dog in the ring, try to see being first in a positive way. Mindy says that she used to hate being first until she decided that it was really a huge advantage because you just walked the course. Going first is great because the course and your planned strategy are still fresh in your mind. Mindy changed her thoughts regarding going first and when she did that, her fear disappeared.

Another way to rid yourself of fear is to use *desensitization.* This process is the same as it would be for a fearful dog you are training. If you are working with a dog that is afraid of the seesaw, you would come up with a plan to systematically break down the process of doing the seesaw into very small pieces. The idea would be that the small parts of doing the seesaw would not cause the dog a great deal of anxiety. You can use Susan Garrett's technique of teaching the seesaw. By placing a 30-inch table under the down part of the seesaw, you make pivoting the seesaw a lot easier. Then slowly you ask the dog to pivot the seesaw more, by shortening the legs on the table. Eventually the dog is doing the seesaw with no problems, because you set up the dog for success.

Do the same thing with your fear in terms of competition. First, make it only a little fear for you to overcome. Then slowly "lower the table" and then begin to phase it out completely.

Another option regarding fear is just to do it anyway. This is called *flooding*. Flooding is when you are fearful of something and you simply do it anyway. If you use flooding, you should only use it on yourself. Never flood a student or a dog.

I feel fear when

I can prevent this by

My plan, when I feel fear, is to... List the steps you will take to either ignore the fear, change your perspective like Mindy Lytle did, or systematically desensitize yourself.

Nancy Gyes recalls that when she first started showing her young Border Collie Riot she was very nervous and excited because the dog is so fast. Now the seasoned team has gone on to many accomplishments, including the 1999 USDAA national championship in the 22-inch division.

PHOTO BY TIEN TRAN.

### Fear Fantasy

You can fear that the dog will run out of the ring. You can fear that the dog will refuse a jump. You can fear that the dog will stop and sniff everything, or you can *stop* giving fear so much power. What is the worst thing that could happen if your fear comes true? A handler has never been kidnapped by aliens while running a course. In the larger scheme of things, will this run really matter? Find out *specifically* what it is that seems scary. Then indulge yourself in your fear fantasy.

If your fear fantasy is that your dog goes off-course, then pretend you are running a course and your dog goes off-course... *so what?* Everybody laughs? You do not qualify? Big deal. Do not give your fear any power. What is the worst thing that will happen if your fear comes true? If you are fearful your dog will stop and sniff on course, develop a "so-what" attitude. The more you worry about this the more likely it will occur.

## Thoughts About Your Teammate

People spend a great deal of time watching and participating in team sports. We learn to be part of a team when we are little kids. We learn about doing what is best for the team. We learn about team spirit and good sportsmanship. Then we become agility handlers and make a mistake. We begin to think of our dogs and ourselves as a team in the human sense. Well, a dog and a person are a *unique* team, because one of the team members is a dog and not another person. Dogs did not spend time in kindergarten learning how to be part of a team and what good sportsmanship is. They are pack animals and pack behavior does not include agility. A dog's idea of teamwork is making a kill or tugging back and forth with another dog over a carcass, so it only makes sense to treat the dog and handler team as a unique team. Being a unique team means that while you need the dog to actually perform the obstacles, you are responsible for *everything*.

What complicates the teamwork further is that our dogs do not speak English. It is impossible to tell a dog ahead of time what lies ahead in the course and how you would like him to handle it. Your team member cannot understand the word "tunnel," she can only associate that sound with "that long round thing." The challenge and the joy of the dog and handler team lies in the test of your signal, verbal and body language.

The fact that dogs cannot be members of a team like people can is good news. This means you do not ever have to feel like you let down your teammate or that she let you down. Thinking that your dog let you down is a humanization of the dog and is therefore not accurate. So if your dog makes a mistake, you do not have to take it personally, you only need to get back to training and fix the problem.

### Struggling or Being Frustrated with Your Dog

*"Dogs do not resist us without reason, they do not resist us just to resist us."*

—Patty Ruzzo

Below write a statement that describes the struggle or frustration that you are experiencing with your dog. Include thoughts that you have while you are struggling or frustrated. Make sure to describe all aspects of the dog. Tell the dog's story. Write it as if you were a tour guide taking someone on a guided tour of your dog and your training struggle/frustration.

An example would be: *My dog is always unfocused in the ring. My dog punishes me for my handling errors by taking off-course obstacles. I cannot get my dog to like agility. She always runs out of the ring before the end of the course.*

Now, read what you have written. Underline any negative, hopeless, unconstructive, unhelpful statements. Please redo the entire exercise described above, but this time with the struggle expressed as a challenge. The frustration becomes something that *used to* be a problem, but you are well on your way to resolving it.

As an example, the reworded passage from above would now read: *My dog has a tendency to become unfocused in the ring, but I am working hard to help her be more focused both in and out of the ring. I am also working on my own focus. I am teaching my dog better attention. I am doing this by playing the name game: I say her name and she looks at me. I play this game with her for five minutes several times a day. I am also rewarding my dog whenever she looks at me on her own. When competing, my dog gets confused easily and it is very important for me to help her be clear about what I am asking her to do. I am working on teaching my dog to love agility. I am doing this by pairing fun things with obstacles so that the obstacle, by association with the fun toy, will become fun itself. By doing this I will soon be able to prevent her from leaving the ring before we have completed the course.*

Finally, take a moment and see the future for you and this dog. See yourself and your dog with the struggle gone and the frustration evaporated. See how you now dance around courses together. Describe your *new* and *improved* vision for this dog. Remember, if you do not believe in your dog, no one will! Pati Hatfield says, *"If you always run your dog like he is a slow dog, he will always be a slow dog."* See your dog racing around the course with you. Or calling off every tunnel or whatever it is you need to see to believe in your dog. Describe how you and your dog will soon be running courses below.

For example: *I can see my dog loving agility and being sad when our practice sessions are over. I can see us running courses and loving every minute. At the end of our runs, I can see my dog smiling, mouth open and tongue hanging.*

The goal of this exercise is to help you break out of the frustration cycle and develop a new vision for you and your dog. Please note that this entire exercise is challenging. If you find yourself stuck and unable to reword your struggle in a positive way, have a friend or your instructor help you.

A smiling dog, Maggie, doing the tunnel.

PHOTO BY JANE LEGARD.

## Questions to Ask Yourself

| | |
|---|---|
| 1. When you are in the show ring or about to enter the ring, what are your typical thoughts? | |
| 2. Analyze the above thoughts and replace each thought that is not helpful with a positive one. | |
| 3. After a non-qualifying run, what are your thoughts? | |
| 4. When reviewing what you have written above, note any negative thoughts and reword them below: | |
| 5. In the past, when you were competing, what types of thoughts were helpful to you? List them below and use these thoughts. | |
| 6. What types of thoughts were *not* helpful? List them below and replace them with positive statements. | |
| 7. What types of thoughts were helpful while training your dog? | |
| 8. In the past, when you were training your dog, what types of thoughts were *not* helpful? For each negative thought, list a new helpful thought. | |
| 9. In general, who will be a better trainer, someone who has experienced training challenges or someone who has not? | |

# Chapter 5

## *Focus*

*Worrying will only divert my focus from the task at hand.*
*When it is all over I am still going home with my dog*
*to lead an ordinary life, no one remembers our outstanding*
*achievements, as they will not remember the ones in which*
*we blew up. We have done our homework and everything*
*will go according to plan. I trust my dog to do its part,*
*just run it out, and do the dance. I focus, so my*
*teammate can follow my lead.*

—Katie Greer

Focus is the ability to zero in on one activity and block out everything else. Monica Percival says that people who don't know her will initially think she is rude, because when she is just about to go in the ring she does not speak to anyone or make eye contact with people around her. If she is approached by someone, she will try to ignore the person and continue warming up the dog and reviewing the course. Monica is not being rude, she is focusing. She has zeroed in on her run and any conversation would break her concentration and destroy the focus she has established.

What helps you focus and the exact method of how you do focus will depend on you. For some people, talking about the course and brainstorming handling options helps get them very focused. For other people, this method may cause them to lose focus because they did not spend enough quiet time walking and memorizing the course.

When you find the method that works for you, apply it, even if people think you are being rude. After your run you can socialize and, if you choose to, you can explain why you prefer not to talk prior to your runs.

## How We Concentrate

Research shows that before an athlete begins a peak performance his mind actually goes blank. Brain scans show that there is very little brain activity and the activity that is occurring is very focused. The same is true for agility com-

Linda Mecklenburg says that the extra pressure of a serious competition, such as running her young Border Collie Awesome in the 1999 USDAA Steeplechase Championships, gives her the adrenaline she needs to be extremely focused.

Photo by Ardis Lukens.

petitors, because when I asked top competitor Pati Hatfield what she thinks of before she goes in the ring her immediate response was "*Nothing!*"

Some of us are able to concentrate better than others; however, the great thing is that everybody can learn to concentrate extremely well under pressure. Linda Mecklenburg is blessed with that ability to concentrate well even under pressure. In fact, the extra pressure of a serious competition gives her the adrenaline she needs to be extremely focused. The extra pressure pushes her into her peak performance Zone.

Lori Lewis, who competes in agility with her two Labradors, had a focus problem with one of her Labs. Lori explained, *"One of the BEST lessons that I ever learned about my handling was how much my dog is affected by my nerves. When I am nervous, she will pick up on it and start in with her stress-induced sniffing episodes. Any time I got upset over her running off and sniffing in the ring, it would only serve to fuel the fire. Once I settled myself down and FOCUSED on the task at hand, she was much more relaxed and able to concentrate without worrying about doing something wrong."*

Lori describes how her Lab cued off her nerves and got unfocused and sniffed. When Lori was able to concentrate and focus, the sniffing disappeared. This is another example of how much our behavior affects our dogs. They truly take their cues from us, both the cues intended, and the ones not intended. If you focus on the task at hand in the ring and do not allow yourself to be distracted by pressure or nerves, then your dog will be able to focus too.

## Improving Your Focus

Regardless of whether you are like Linda Mecklenburg or whether you have a hard time focusing, you can use the following techniques to improve your focus.

### Clear Your Mind

Learn to think about nothing on command. If thinking of nothing does not work, focus on one thing only. Something like watching your dog. You can help clear your mind by imagining that every thought you have is inside a bubble that is slowly drifting away. You can also use this when you overhear other competitors making negative comments. You take the negative comment, "This competition is chaos," stick it in a bubble, and let it drift away. This prevents you from being programmed with junk comments that you accidentally overhear. You must avoid negative thoughts because they will act as a distraction and destroy your concentration. You must have your "negative-thought-seeking missile" fully armed and immediately ready to fire when you hear or accidentally think a negative thought.

STUART MAH describes some of the techniques he used that helped him get in the Zone while at the 1996 World Championships: *"I usually decide that rather than just trying to qualify, I will try to focus or concentrate on having the best run that the dog and I can possibly ever have, and have fun while doing it. At the World Championships in 1996, I was the alternate dog so I did not have to run team, but I was running individuals. I decided after the first day that I did not care if my dog won. I just set an attitude that I want to run the absolutely very best that I can to show that it can be done, but I did not necessarily care if I won. We ended up in second place in Standard agility out of 102 dogs, only a second or so out of first."*

By focusing on doing the best that he and his dog could do Stuart freed himself of pressure and this enabled him to perform in the Zone. Stuart chose only two things to focus on: 1) doing the best that he and the dog could; and 2) having fun.

In equestrian events, top competitors hire individuals to assist them to get their horses ready. The specific tasks that the assistant engages in depend on the competitor, but usually the assistant cleans the horse, braids the horse's mane, and makes sure the animal is fed and watered. Consider recruiting a friend or family member to assist you with your dogs. If you teach, this is an excellent way to give a "newbie" a behind-the-scenes view of what makes a good run happen. An assistant could cool down a dog you just finished running while you warm up the next. Dogs would love this, since it is much better than being put into a crate without getting a chance to catch their breath. The assistant could also help you with the running order and notify you of scratches while you warm up your dog at the practice jump.

At the 1996 World Championships, Sharon Anderson, in addition to coaching the team, assisted all of the U.S. team members with the running order and timing of their warm-ups. Jane Simmons-Moake says that this enabled her to truly concentrate on what she needed to, and was part of the reason that she and Holly were able to Zone during their run.

Jane put it this way, *"Another factor in reaching the Zone was being able to concentrate entirely on my dog before we ran. Coach Sharon Anderson helped keep track of the order of who was running, when we should enter the staging area, and how many dogs were left before we ran. Without this responsibility, I was free to concentrate on my dog and our warm-up routine completely."*

Both Stuart and Jane give examples of how they were able to use different methods to have the focus that they needed to succeed at the highest level of competition. These are examples of how you can stay focused despite the excitement and intense pressure of a World Championship.

### Select a Concentration Word

Pick a word that helps you focus, like "one" or "smooth." It needs to be a very simple word that you can easily repeat to yourself. Do not use a phrase since this could be distracting. The idea is to program yourself to focus intensely when you are repeating this word to yourself.

For Jane Simmons-Moake, one factor in reaching the Zone is being able to concentrate entirely on her dog Holly before she runs.

PHOTO BY BILL NEWCOMB.

Experiment with using your concentration word in training first before you use it in competition. What word do you think would work well for you?

### Use Humor to Refocus

If you get distracted by a handling error, try using humor to refocus. Humor is a great tool. Practice laughing to relieve stress. Write down things that are funny and use this list when you need a good laugh.

A handler who was competing with a young retriever demonstrated an example of using humor to cope with a run. It seems that the dog was very revved up before his run. During his run, the dog saw one of the orange course marker cones and picked it up. The retriever's handler attempted to get the dog to drop it, but when she was unable to, decided to make the best of the situation and have the dog finish the course with the cone in his mouth. The retriever completed the rest of the course, including the chute and the weave poles, with the cone in his mouth. The handler laughed as much as the crowd and ended up having a very fun run despite the "cone incident."

Initially when the handler realized that the dog had picked up the cone she experienced a major distraction. However, the retriever's handler did a great job of just allowing the humor of this situation to help her get refocused and complete the run, making it a positive experience for herself and her dog.

## Focus in Competition

Nancy Gyes has developed an intense ability to focus in competition through "*years of practice at concentrating, and maybe more importantly, confidence in my dogs and my own level of training and ability.*" Clearly Nancy's ability to focus and her confidence are intertwined. For Nancy, and for most people, both focus and confidence are important Zone factors that are dependent on each other.

> MARQ CHEEK describes his most-focused and least-focused runs like this: "*Now that I am over my pre-run jitters, since I have been competing for several years, I have been able to analyze when I perform best. Personally when I really want or need a leg, I stay in better focus. There have been several USDAA Masters Standard legs that, recently, I did not earn, because I really did not need them after getting the MAD title and I mentally sloughed off their importance. As a consequence, I did not prepare well enough and I did not study the runs performed before mine for 'real-time' training.*"
>
> For Marq, focus and some pressure are important Zone factors. Marq goes on to say, "*On the other end of the spectrum, I have noticed that when I go 'all out' and try to win a class outright, that I overdo it and force errors. My best performances have come when I step up to the line with a plan I am convinced will work after studying all options intently. I take a deep breath or two and tell myself 'we can do everything on this course.' I remember playing softball (my sport before agility) and I was most successful at the plate when I said to myself 'they are not going to get me out.' Migrating that*

*thought to agility—'This course is ours, it is not going to get us.' I like to think of my dog as Mr. Consistent. He is not the fastest dog out there, but cumulatively over a series of competitions he will have more victories as a result of being fairly quick and quite reliable."*

Focus can only occur when other Zone factors are in place. If you are concerned that your dog may be lacking skills to successfully conquer a course she is running, you will be unable to focus.

What factors need to be in place for you to focus at a competition?

## Your Dog and Focus

Have you ever had a dog go around a course with you while sniffing? Or have you had a dog stop at the top of the A-frame and just stare at the landscape? Dogs need to learn to focus just as we do. If you do not train your dog to focus even with distractions, then it is unreasonable for you to expect your dog to focus in competition. Teaching your dog obedience exercises such as a heel with attention will greatly improve your dog's ability to focus.

The following are some common signals that your dog is not focusing:

- Sniffing
- Wandering
- Getting distracted
- Running out of the ring
- Slowing down when she used to run fast
- Herding and biting

The most important factor here is to listen to your dog. Rather than viewing these behaviors as irritating, try to understand what your dog is attempting to communicate to you. Dogs run agility courses at high speed very successfully for nothing but our love and the enjoyment of the sport. Why then would they want to torture us with resistance? You need to view resistance as important information for training, rather than as a deliberate, spiteful act on the dog's part. Most importantly, you must always rule out medical issues.

Before you begin focus training with your dog, take an assessment of what behavior your dog is displaying when she is distracted or lacking focus. Dogs display most of the behaviors listed above as the result of stress or frustration. Take a look at the following example.

## *Example*

Suppose your dog is sniffing. What is the dog trying to communicate to you? Communication with your dog is not a one-way street. Dogs try to tell us stuff, too. According to Turid Rugaas, author of *Calming Signals*, sniffing is a calming signal. A calming signal is a dog's way of saying, "Peace, I mean no harm." Of course, Turid also says that you have to see the sniffing to be sure what is going on in each specific situation. It seems very likely that sniffing in agility training or competition is likely to be related to stress. The solution is simple:

1. Evaluate why the dog is stressing and identify the stress triggers.
2. Begin to reinforce the dog for not sniffing and focusing.
3. Gradually expose the dog to the stress triggers.

These are common sources for dog stress:

- The dog is underprepared for competition (for example, sequences are more complicated than she has been trained for).
- The dog is overwhelmed by the smells and noises of competition because her training has not been proofed.
- The dog has not had enough rest or is sick.
- The dog is hungry or thirsty.
- You are not communicating clearly with your dog.

The most common source for dog stress is not communicating clearly with your dog. If you question this, just take your dog up to some agility equipment and start consistently signaling one obstacle with your body and another with your voice. See how long it takes for your dog to start showing signs of stress. You can also try repeating the commands for each obstacle about five times, or calling them in a different tone of voice than you do in practice. Or, start signaling with frantic and jerky body movements. All these things will cause your dog to eventually show signs of stress, and when she does, she might sniff or engage in other unwanted behaviors.

One way to guard against miscommunication is to routinely videotape both practice and competition runs. This allows you to review your handling and compare your practice handling to your competition handling. The goal is for both the practice and the competition handling to be the same. Doing this will guard against your dog losing focus while on a competition course.

Another idea is to tape the noises at a dog show and then play the tape recording at home while the dog is resting, and, eventually, during training. This way you are teaching your dog to focus despite all the noises and distraction that she hears from the tape. While recording sounds for the tape make sure to set the tape at various locations (such as your tent, the start line, or near barking dogs), or you can even walk around with the tape recorder.

Another helpful strategy is to audiotape your commands. Take a moment to review the Masters Standard course below and think about how you would handle the course and specifically what commands you would say to your dog. Following are two lists of verbal commands for the course in the illustration.

If you were a dog, which handler would you want? Which one is communicating more clearly with her dog? When you audiotape your commands, you will have the opportunity to evaluate how clearly you are communicating with your dog. Lots of words equals clutter. Less is more. The more clutter in your commands, the more likely that your dog will tune you out. Or, the dog may be so busy listening to everything that you are saying that she never opens up her stride and lets it rip. If this sounds like an argument for running silently, it is. If you tend to use many words and repeat your commands, try to run your dog silently and see what happens.

Be sure to gradually change over from cluttered to uncluttered commands while you are competing. Some dogs grow accustomed to your verbal clutter and come to rely on it as comforting, and you want to give this dog a chance to get used to your new, uncluttered vocabulary. You will find that uncluttering your commands is likely to speed up your dog and improve your handling.

Dogs that ran novice courses with great speed only to slow down at the upper levels are usually being overhandled. Another aspect of verbal clutter is that it will not help your dog in terms of learning verbal discrimination of the obstacles. The power of verbal discrimination is when you only have to say it one time. By repeating the commands you are actually "untraining" verbal discrimination.

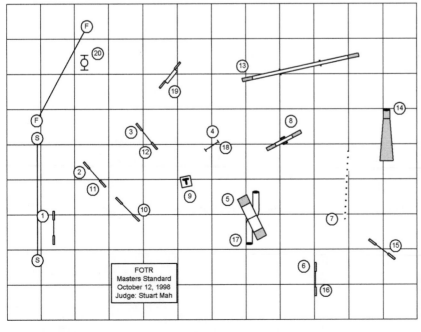

**List One**

Stay, Stay, Stay, Stay, Stay, Stay, Jump, Jump, Jump, Heeeeeeeere, Here, Here, Jump, Charge, Charge, Charge, Bottom, Bottom, Bottom, Jump, Weeeeeave, Weave, Weave, Weave, Weave, Heeeerrrre, Teeter, Bottom, Bottom, Bottom, Table, Table, Table, Table, Jump, Here, Here, Here, Jump, Jump, Walk, Walk It, Go Walk, Come on hurry up, Hurry, Hurry, Bottom, Bottom, Bottom, Here, Chute, Jump, Jump, Go out, Go out, Go out, Tunnel, Tunnel, Tunnel, Jump, Jump, Heeeere, Tire.

**List Two**

Stay, Jump, Jump, Jump, Here, Jump, Charge, Bottom, Jump, Here, Weave, Here, Teeter, Bottom, Go table, Here, Jump, Jump, Jump, Go Walk, Bottom, Here, Chute, Jump, Jump, Tunnel, Jump, Jump, Here, Tire.

This dog turns back to herd the handler and tell her that she needs to hurry up and tell him where to go next.

PHOTO BY KATHY PEPIN.

Finally, consider that verbal clutter may actually be reinforcing your dog for making an incorrect decision. For example, at the A-frame/tunnel discrimination your dog mistakenly heads for the A-frame and the "clutter-command-handler" starts screaming, "Tunnel, tunnel, tunnel;" since the dog has already been untrained regarding verbal obstacle discrimination, the dog interprets the screaming as an encouragement for speed. The result is the dog goes blasting up the A-frame, the incorrect obstacle.

Once you have uncluttered your commands and have established clear verbal communication with your dog it will be time to videotape a run and ensure that your body is also sending clear signals.

A final note on clear communication regarding the timing and pace of your signals and commands: Agility is about speed. While it may be comfortable to slowly and precisely handle a dog around a course, it will not help you qualify without time faults. Many unfocused behaviors that dogs exhibit are directly linked to the speed of your signals. This is especially true for dogs that bark at or herd their handlers. Your verbal communication might be clear, but if you are running a high-drive dog, this may not be enough. Speed is what some of these dogs want. If they do not get the commands early, these dogs will make up their own course, demand bark at you, or bite and herd you. For these dogs, it is imperative to signal as fast as possible. This means both verbal and body signals must be fired out very rapidly. This type of dog will not be willing to match your pace, but rather you must match the pace of the dog. This is one reason that Stuart Mah says that a fast dog and a slow handler are the most difficult combination. Regardless of the type of dog and handler combination, we can all learn to call and signal obstacles fast and early.

For dogs that are not high-drive, the speed of the signals is equally important. Successful handling is about clarity of the commands, timing, and speed of the commands. If you want to finish courses at warp speed, you need to be signaling at warp speed.

## Top Competitors on Keeping Your Dog Focused

If your dog is lacking focus in training or in competition, you can easily fix this. Bud Houston, Pati Hatfield, and Katie Greer have some advice for you.

> BUD HOUSTON says that if you want to keep your dog focused while training and competing, then *"The dog's handler should be more interesting than the ground."* Bud's comment is humorous and simple, but very true.

> PATI HATFIELD explains, *"It really comes down to being a good trainer. Teaching your dog to focus is a learned behavior just like anything else. All too often the emphasis is on trying to get a dog who is not focused to do so. Instead it should be a proactive approach to teaching the dog to focus so the behavior is there when you need it."*

If your dog is not focusing, do not blame the dog for not paying attention. Ask yourself how many times you have reinforced your dog for being focused. Sometimes competitors forget to reward the most basic behaviors. Focus can be one of them.

> KATIE GREER says to help a dog have good focus in the ring and in training, *"Handlers need to make sure that they are interesting to the dog. Some need to be more animated while working with their dogs, both visually and vocally. They can work on this away from the obstacles with lots of play training. Many dogs can become convinced that some toys are actually fun if the handler experiments with them and does not give up too soon. Put everything up and only allow them to play with you, not on their own. Find opportunities to show the dog that you are more interesting. Take them to places filled with other people. Sometimes allow them the freedom to do as they wish and break it up with periods of attention on some task at hand. Loading up on tricks to perform goes a long way with this. Can you down, can you bark, can you spin, can you high five… there is a very long list of possibilities. Clicker work really turns on most dogs as it gives them some control in the game. They enjoy working on getting their handlers to make that sound and earn the reward. For just a few minutes and a couple of dollars, this is a very good play session for everyone."*

Tricks can be a great way to get a dog focused on you before going into the ring. Dog trainer and behaviorist, Donna Duford, has written a book called *Agility Tricks*, which is dedicated to the subject of doing trick training with agility dogs for the purposes of improving focus and attention as well as flexibility. Often, a distracted dog can be re-focused on you by asking him to perform a simple trick.

Do some dogs have attention deficit disorder? Probably, but just like people, even dogs with extreme distraction issues can learn to focus. As with other training, some dogs will learn more quickly than others. By beginning with rewarding for basic eye contact, you can train any dog to focus. Another useful technique is teaching the dog to check in after each obstacle. Finally,

If you teach your dog tricks, you can use them as part of your pre-run ritual to get the dog focused on you and working with you.

Photo by Sue Sternberg.

you should never permit high-drive dogs that love agility to do any of the obstacles on their own as this is a very fast way to untrain any handler focus the dog may have had.

If keeping focus is difficult for your dog, consider

- rewarding for eye contact, and slowly increasing to longer and longer periods of time.
- developing a fantastic recall.
- playing lots of games that require a human partner to be fun. Tug is a good one.
- training your dog to perform a competition heel with attention, on-side and off-side.
- spending a lot of time practicing call-offs. Make this a fun game. Katie Greer calls this the fake-out game.

## Questions to Ask Yourself

There are many ways to explore concentration. Below you will be asked questions that will help you explore how you might use humor to help yourself refocus, how you have focused in the past, and how you might improve your focus in the future.

| | |
|---|---|
| **1. What is the funniest thing that has ever happened to you?** | |
| **2. What is the funniest agility run you have ever seen?** | |
| **3. What is the funniest thing your dog ever did?** | |
| **4. How about the funniest thing your dog ever did in the agility ring?** | |

Shamelessly exploit the humor above and use it when you need to cheer yourself up, or distract yourself, or when you need to refocus on fun.

5. Think back to a time when you were extremely focused. What helped you get into that focused state of mind?

6. What was your body doing?

7. What did you notice about your dog?

8. What things have prevented you from focusing when you needed to?

9. How can you control these things in the future?

10. What might be helpful to experiment with?

## Chapter 6

# *Visualize*

*What you see, you can be.*

*Visualization* is the technique of running a mental videotape of something that you

- would like to accomplish.
- have done in the past.
- are interested in practicing.

When you run the mental videotape, you can strengthen the image you are seeing by describing what you see aloud and tape recording it or by writing it down. Another way to do this is to tell someone what you are visualizing. The only limit to this visualization stuff is your imagination and trial and error in terms of what works and does not work for you.

Take a moment to examine how visualization has worked for you in the past. Describe the last time you used visualization and what happened as a result:

If the visualization process was not successful for you, please consider trying it again. Visualization does not come naturally to everyone. Regardless of whether you immediately benefited from it or not, you can learn to use visualization and make it work for you.

Below write your opinion of visualization:

Regardless of your opinion, are you willing to have an open mind and work on learning how to visualize? If yes, please continue reading. If no, please skip to the next chapter.

## Visualization Guidelines

1. Practice visualizing on a regular basis.
2. Do not begin visualizing at a competition unless you know how you will react to the visualization process.
3. Use all of your senses to enhance visualization; hear, see, smell, feel, and taste your visualization.
4. Develop control over your visualization. Practice visualization until you can control all aspects of the content of what you are "seeing." Do not allow any negatives to enter into your visualization, and if they do, resolve them positively. When you have control over your visualization, you will be able to speed up and slow down what you are visualizing. If you visualize your run before you are in the ring, but speed it up to twice as fast as your dog will actually run it, you will have the impression of having all the time in the world while actually running your dog.
5. Visualize both internal and external perspectives. This means see yourself running the course as if you are a spectator, and also see yourself running the course as if you are the handler. Videotapes are very helpful for you to develop the skill of visualizing yourself running from the external perspective.
6. Enhance visualization by adding relaxation. According to Gould and Damarjian in *Sports and Exercise Psychology*, visualization done in combination with relaxation is much more effective than imagery alone.
7. Use visualization to prepare for the unexpected change in running order or to learn fast recovery from handling errors.
8. Use visualization in practice before using it in competition.

## Developing Your Ability for Visualization

Visualization does not come naturally to everyone. The following sections discuss techniques you can use to help you improve your ability to visualize.

### Mental Target Training

Make sure you have a clear mental picture of what it is you wish to train your dog to do. If you want 2.5 second weave poles, make sure that you know what your dog will look like when she is doing it. This gives you a mental target.

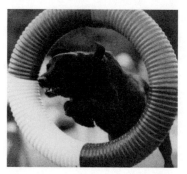

Visualization gives you a mental target of where you want to go, just like a tire is a target to a leaping dog.

PHOTO BY TIEN TRAN.

Just as you might give a dog a Plexiglas target to "touch" at the bottom of the contacts, a mental target helps you know where you are heading. If your dog has a problem with speed, picture her running a course fast. Now see her running it even faster. Now store that picture on your mental VCR cassette and replay it as much as possible. Replay it when you are sitting at a red light in your car. Replay it when you are on your lunch break. Replay it when you are going to sleep at night.

If you are having a hard time visualizing your dog running fast, watch her chasing a squirrel in the backyard, then use that visual for your mental videotape of her running a course very, very fast.

## Imagination

Let us say that you dream of showing at the USDAA National Finals. Use your imagination to see, hear, smell, touch, taste, and emotionally feel what it will be like when you are there. Make sure to include all of your senses.

The National Finals will look like

Sound like

Smell like

Feel like

Taste like (Salty air? Or food from the banquet?)

Emotionally I will be

What would you eat? What would you think? Use your imagination to make your dream real. This exercise will help you feel more comfortable and keep your show nerves at a manageable level. Why wait until your dream happens—start living it now!

### Using Your Imagination to Problem Solve

If you tripped and fell the last time you were competing, and you are now concerned with this happening again, consider using your imagination to visualize falling and then making a great recovery and barely losing any time. Use visualization to make the best out of any situation.

Using visualization for problem solving also gives you the opportunity to evaluate what it was that caused you to trip. In your mind, you run the mental video of when you tripped over and over. Each time you look for more information. Were you dragging your feet? Did you trip over a stake? Was your shoelace untied? Understanding what caused the problem can then help you solve it and usually prevent it from happening again.

A big part of using visualization as a training technique is to anticipate everything and anything that could possibly go wrong and to find a positive resolution for it. It is about brainstorming the possibilities of what could happen and what you would do. In the book *Sports Psyching*, the author describes an Olympic competitor who liked to listen to a certain tape before competing. One day she forgot her tape. She and her coach had brainstormed regarding this possibility; the competitor had visualized forgetting the tape and decided that if this happened, she would sing the song to herself. This ended up working so well that she never went back to actually playing the tape.

### Same and Similar

Visualization is so powerful that frequently your mind cannot tell the difference between what you have visualized and what has actually happened. This is very good news to the agility competitor who enjoys using visualization. The fact that your mind cannot distinguish same and similar enables you to use visualization to run the course before you actually ever set foot on it with your dog.

But wait, you are visualizing clean runs and what if your dog swings wide and heads for the wrong obstacle? You can use visualization to correct the problem. Before you run, come up with a plan. What if "Nitro" heads for the tunnel instead of the jump? Your plan is to tuck your shoulder and pull hard. You can now use visualization to test drive your handling ideas.

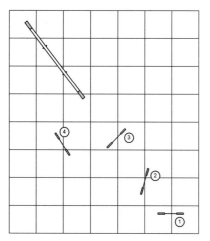

For example, at obstacle #3 you encounter a very challenging trap. You are concerned that your dog might take the off-course to the dogwalk instead of the correct obstacle, a jump, which is #4. Visualizing your dog doing the sequence you "see" him heading for the incorrect obstacle. You also visualize yourself calling him off the dogwalk and redirecting him to the correct jump. The final step is to rewind your mental videotape to the point where you can prevent the error. Add the directional command at the correct moment to prevent the dog from even looking at the dogwalk.

Now you have the benefit of having already run your dog on the course and seen how she might react and you have fixed your handling. Your brain is unable to distinguish between same and similar, and it will actually think you have already run the course. Voila, a clean run!

## Use Visualization for...

- teaching yourself footwork such as the front cross, rear cross, or blind cross.
- getting a clear picture of what your goal is (for example, how what you want your dog to do will look).
- mentally programming your handling movements for your next run.
- creating a mental picture of having fun with your dog, and your dog giving you that special "happy face."

Whatever you decide to visualize, the key is repetition. Research shows that we actually learn to do movements by watching other competitors. This is learning by mimicry. If you watch a run by a super handler, make sure to continue visualizing what you saw. This will ensure that you will be able to mimic the movements. Another way to do this is to use video. Once you have repeatedly watched the same video you will be able to recall the movements that you saw and run them on your mental video camera.

Once you develop the mental video visualization skill you can use it to review your run after the fact. Mindy Lytle, a top competitor from Florida, advises handlers to review the runs that they had during the day. Mindy explains that you can use the method of visualizing the run you had earlier that day to assess what you have learned and to focus on the positive.

One competitor that used Mindy's reviewing technique said it was very helpful to her. The competitor explained that she had been doing great with her dog all weekend. Then in the last class on the last day of competition the dog went off-course. After the competitor left the ring with her dog, some spectators commented that her dog simply ignored her recall command. The competitor said that somehow she did not feel satisfied with this conclusion. So she reviewed her mental videotape of the run and realized that she had never made the turn with her body. Being unsure of whether this had really occurred, she reviewed the real videotape and, sure enough, she had just stood there facing the off-course obstacle while saying "Here." Like Jane Simmons-Moake points out in her video, "*Check your feet*" when an error has occurred. Checking your feet is one way to know if you are out of position.

By sending the dog conflicting signals, body signaling the off-course while verbally calling "Here," the competitor had accidentally caused the off-course. Because visualization helped her be aware of this, she can now train better and avoid this handling problem in the future.

Mindy's idea of visualizing the run after it has occurred is a win/win technique, because you are either building your confidence by reviewing a clean run or learning how to avoid handling errors in the future.

Bud Houston has a unique way of using visualization. Several days before a competition he begins visualizing clean runs. When at the competition and while walking the course, he visualizes how fast the dog will be going and where the dog will be. He then uses this information to plan his strategy. He says that he will even visualize himself working the contact because "*that is what I will be doing.*"

## Potential Problems with Visualization

Keep your eyes peeled for the following, which can lead to problems with using visualization:

- **Unrealistic expectations**—visualization is not a quick fix. It is a skill that takes practice and time to develop.
- **Lack of practice**—visualization will work for everyone. Some handlers will naturally be more into visualization than others, but visualization will benefit every competitor who practices this skill.

If you do not know how you are going to respond to visualization, do not experiment with it in competition. One competitor told me about how she disliked visualization and will never use it again, because the one time she used it she visualized a clean run and then went in the ring and completely blew her run. When the competitor analyzed what had happened, the competitor realized that she had accidentally created a ton of pressure to handle perfectly by visualizing a clean run. The competitor continued to experiment with visualization and found that when she used visualization to help her memorize the course, it did not cause her to feel pressured and that it assisted her greatly in improving her competition handling.

So, if you have had a bad experience using visualization, give visualization a second chance.

## Visualization and Injuries

Agility is a sport. Both handlers and dogs can experience injuries. The more you learn and practice using visualization, the more skilled you become. Should either you or your dog experience an injury, you will be able to continue running agility mentally. One injured handler told me how she continued to go to shows even though she was unable to run. She would walk the course and strategize as if she were running her dog. She would memorize the course and then she would go to her tent and watch other handlers run. After her injury healed, she noticed that many of the training problems she had been experiencing with her dog had disappeared. Initially this puzzled her. Later she realized that she had been training and running her dog mentally. While she was unable to perform physically, her agility handling skills actually improved.

Jane Savoie, the author of *That Winning Feeling*, explains how she used visualization to practice her dressage patterns when she did not have the time to ride her horse and practice as much as she needed to. The surprise ending to her visualization story is that Savoie and her horse won a major competition because of her use of visualization, even though they were actually underprepared.

## Questions to Ask Yourself

| | |
|---|---|
| 1. Right now, I am trying to teach my dog the following new skill: | |
| 2. The mental image I have of my dog doing this new skill perfectly is | |
| 3. When you have experimented with visualizing, what has worked? | |
| 4. What type of visualization has not been helpful (be specific)? | |
| 5. If you have been struggling or been frustrated with your dog, use visualization to imagine having fun with your dog. What does it look like when you are having fun with your dog? | |

Now use this information to make this fun real.

## Chapter 7

# *Relax*

*"The Zone requires a balance between relaxation and tension."*

—Diane Tosh

The ability to relax on command and breathe deeply are very important skills. When you stay calm under pressure, it greatly improves your ability to focus. There are many ways to learn to relax discussed in this chapter. As with all the techniques, you will need to experiment with what works best for you. For some competitors it is an important element of Zoning to be relaxed as they enter the ring. For other competitors it is not important.

Bud Houston says that he is "*never relaxed*" when competing. He is quick to add that he also never feels nervous at the start line. He attributes this to his pacing and constant moving, which helps him burn off the nerves before he ever gets close to the start line.

All competitors need to evaluate how they get to the point of relaxation that works best for them.

## Begin with Breathing

Breathe deeply. Put your hand on your stomach and feel your whole abdomen rise as you inhale. Do not hold your breath. Just inhale deeply and exhale. Observe your breathing in different situations. When you are in a hurry and get stuck in rush-hour traffic, how do you breathe? When you are relaxed, how do you breathe? Mimic this normal breathing when you are in competition to help you relax.

Use all different kinds of situations to practice your deep breathing. Combine the deep breathing with relaxing all of your muscles. Remember that you are practicing this because your dog will ultimately cue off your breathing when you are competing in the ring. By learning to control your breathing, you can control and guard against unintentional cueing.

Get completely relaxed and try taking a nap before you compete (make sure to bring and set an alarm). Pati Hatfield has the wonderful ability to nap whenever she needs to. At the 1997 USDAA National Finals, Pati and her dog Lilly, "*watched a few of the 12-inch runs just to see how the course ran and*

Pati Hatfield has the wonderful ability to relax and take a nap whenever she needs to. She recounts napping up until the last possible moment at the 1997 USDAA finals (where she ultimately won the 30-inch division) and then getting out her dog, warming up, and going in the ring.

PHOTO BY BILL NEWCOMB.

*then Lil and I took a nap. We woke up as the 24-inch dogs were halfway through. This left us enough time to warm up and find we were two away from being in."* To see if napping will help you relax, test this idea in practices and matches.

Obedience competitors have been using breathing to cue their dogs for probably as many years as obedience competition has existed. In the Utility class, one exercise requires the handler to put her smell on a special dumbbell by rubbing her hands on it. The dog is then asked to find the scented dumbbell and pick it out from other unscented dumbbells. One Utility competitor tells a story of how she observed a handler hold her breath while scenting the articles. In her nervous state the handler repeatedly rubbed her hands on the dumbbell. This meant that she had scented the dumbbell much more than she ever had in training. The handler was nervous because it was a competition and she usually never held her breath. Needless to say the dog got confused and distracted by so many things being different, and the scenting exercise did not go well.

So just for fun, grab your agility dog and set up a course that is appropriate for your level. Next, hold your breath and run the course. Even if you turn blue, make sure you are still holding your breath as you run. If you have to breathe, gasp for air and then immediately hold your breath again. After the run take note of what happened to your body while you ran.

Did you notice how tight your muscles got? Did you notice all the weird looks you got from your dog? Breathing is the cornerstone of a relaxed run. If you do not want your dog to know you are nervous, begin with breathing.

Sheila Booth in her book *Purely Positive* writes, *"When the owner gets nervous in the ring, breathing becomes rapid and shallow. Just when the dog needs him most, the owner seems to have undergone a total transformation."* Sheila goes on to explain how breathing is reflected in the handler's body language and may even cause twitching or clothes tugging. Sheila concludes, *"Then someone has the nerve to blame the dog for a poor routine. It is always a wonder to me that some dogs hang in there at all."*

From the dog's perspective, something simple like a change in your breathing can communicate a whole lot more than you intend. Shallow breathing can also set you up for feeling frustrated about the dog not performing in the ring like she does in practice.

Patty Ruzzo's audiotape, "Positively Ringwise," goes into detail about how you can improve breathing and actually use breathing to improve obedience performances.

To prevent shallow breathing, you will need to develop a technique that assists you with monitoring your breathing. Below are two ways to do this, but you can be creative and come up with your own.

1. Use a visual image to keep track of your breathing. If your breathing during practice is usually one breath per second, then associate a mental image with the desired rhythm of your breathing. For example, you can imagine breathing into a balloon and then use the visual of the balloon filling up and getting flat again to help you track the rhythm of your breathing.

2. Simply count: one, inhale, two, exhale. Again, you are using the counting to teach yourself the rhythm of your breathing when you are practicing.

You can use either of these techniques to help you duplicate the way you breathe in practice for the competition ring. Anticipate when you will have a few seconds to check in on your breathing and then do so. For example, if you have a small dog, you may have time to check on your breathing while your dog is performing the dogwalk or the table. Finally, if you have had an error already and your run is non-qualifying, you might just use some extra time to work contacts and to monitor your breathing.

When you are aware of your practice breathing style, you can apply this information to running a competition agility course.

- **At the start line:** Breathe deep, relaxed breaths and smile at your dog. Get connected with your dog. Do not power struggle with your dog at the start line. That will get you tense and off on the wrong foot.
- **Opening sequence:** Focus on staying relaxed and keep breathing.
- **The first change of side:** Speed up body movements. Increase breathing rate without holding breath.
- **At the table:** Smile at dog and take deep, relaxing breaths.
- **Last third of course:** Keep smiling, keep breathing at a steady rhythm, and keep handling the dog. Do not let up on your breathing or on your handling until your dog crosses the finish line.

Just as a metronome sets the beat for you while you are playing a musical instrument, breathing sets the beat of your run. Holding your breath sets an impossible beat that leads to "crash and burn" runs. Rhythmic and relaxed breathing is the winning ticket.

## Control Your Voice

Once, while judging, I noticed how most competitors began to shout at their dogs as soon as an error occurred. It was as if being louder would somehow help the dog respond. The scenario was something like this: Dog runs beautiful opening sequence while handler calls commands to dog in a normal tone of voice. Then dog runs by the next obstacle and handler begins yelling at the dog with a tense "*Come! Come!*" The interesting part is that every single dog responded to the change in the handler's tone of voice in the exact same way. All dogs that were being yelled at by handlers began sniffing and wandering. This in turn caused the handler to get even louder. It appeared as if the yelling flipped a switch and set the dog into tracking mode.

Needless to say, the handlers with the "agility-tracking dogs" had an even harder time getting their dogs back once the sniffing and wandering behavior was in full force. No one but a dog can say for sure what this sniffing and wandering indicated, but a good guess is that all these dogs were stressing.

If your dog has a sniffing or wandering problem in the ring, you may want to experiment with controlling your voice. You must control both tone and volume to prevent the dog's stress reaction. An important element of controlling tone and volume is breathing. If you respond to a dog's error by holding your breath, this habit will most definitely affect the tone and volume of your commands. You can swap out the holding-your-breath habit for a new habit of rhythmic and relaxed breathing.

Psychologically speaking, you will also benefit from keeping stress and anxiety out of your voice. No matter how hard you concentrate on the course, you will still hear yourself shouting. Shouting is stressful to you, even when you are the one doing the shouting. Stress can cause overarousal and bump you out of the Zone. Shouting will also affect your focus and breathing. If you eliminate shouting, you will automatically improve your focus and breathing.

Top competitors like Stuart Mah and Susan Garrett, to name only two, are almost silent handlers. Stuart's and Susan's dogs are not getting stressed because the tone and volume of the voices they are hearing are soft and relaxed. In addition, Stuart and Susan are having a soothing effect on themselves by handling quietly and smoothly. This does not mean that everyone should be a quiet handler, but if you have a tendency to get tense you may want to explore handling quietly as Stuart and Susan do.

## Center Yourself

Athletes have used centering to aid relaxation for a long time. *Centering* involves becoming very aware of your feet on the ground, and then centering your entire body above your feet. This gives you a physically relaxed and centered starting point. Using centering is great, because it does not take long. Centering can be done very quickly while you are setting your dog at the start line. You could sit him down and then take a couple of seconds to feel the ground below your feet and center yourself before you start your round.

## Use Your Imagination to Relax

A lot of people imagine lying on the beach and hearing the waves, and it is very relaxing to them. Understanding what is relaxing to you will help you select the right "place" for you to visit when you want to relax. This technique is best to use when you are feeling overaroused. If you are feeling more nervous than usual, you want to stop and take a minute to visit your favorite place and relax.

What place would be relaxing to you?

|  |
|  |

What does this place look like? Sound like? Feel like?

|  |
|  |

## Develop Positive Self-Talk

Use positive self-talk to help you relax. "*This is fun.*" Agility competitor Kathy Schrimpf tells herself, "*This is a great course, just the way we like it.*" This helps her get relaxed and focused, and maintain a positive attitude. According to sports psychologist Richard Cox, "*An anxious mind cannot exist in a relaxed body.*"

Nancy Gyes has mastered the skill of positive self-talk. When you listen to how she describes how she found the balance of a little nervous but not too much, you can hear that she is kind with herself. Positive self-talk is just that, being kind to yourself. Nancy says, *"Getting show nerves is actually part of what makes me a better competitor. There have been a few times in national competitions where I have felt relaxed, and was nonchalant about the performance soon to come. I was not successful in completing those rounds cleanly, or with the kind of performance I expect of myself and my dog. There have also been times where I felt like my nerves have gotten the best of me, and I have let them dictate my run. There are always going to be times where you feel less than motivated before a round, or a little 'over the top' like a wild Border Collie. But generally I keep my nerves in rein by focusing on the job at hand, and enjoying the excitement of the moment. It is normal and good to be serious enough about competition that you get a bit of the jitters. The trick is not letting them take over and ruin your day!"*

> Nancy goes on to say, *"I tell myself to calm down and then begin the visualization practice of the elements required before each run. Sometimes I have to literally get tough with myself and remind myself this is SUPPOSED to be fun and challenging, not overwhelming. I try to think about what my dog must think if I act uptight. It cannot be fun for him. If he is not excited and interested, and if he is going to worry about my mental state, he is not going to react like I think he will at every given moment of the test."*

If you do not like the idea of using positive self-talk, do it for your dog.

## Use a Keyword to Trigger Relaxation

You can use a word and condition yourself to relax when you repeat it to yourself. Experiment with using the following words to trigger a relaxation response: breathe, glass, loose, relax, calm, easy, trust.

Begin using the word at home, then use it at work, and slowly build up to tenser situations. Then begin using it in agility practice, progress to a match, and, if all of this has been successful, use the word in competition.

## Make a Good Luck Charm

Choose an object that you would like to have as your good luck charm. Next, hold this object in your hand and get yourself in a very deep state of relaxation. What you want to do is anchor your good luck charm to the feeling of deep relaxation. This is called *pairing*. You will then condition yourself to become very relaxed when you touch your good luck charm. Do not expect this to happen quickly. Spend a lot of time anchoring the relaxation to the good luck charm.

If you are interested in making a good luck charm for yourself, you can use the script in the following section to help you get very relaxed while you hold or rub your good luck charm. Remember that the charm has no power; this is only a technique to assist you in relaxing. If you get to a competition and realize you have forgotten your charm, you can use any object that you have handy. The good luck charm is not lucky, rather the act of rubbing it and relaxing is what helps a tense handler get in the Zone. Consider making the good luck charm a leash or collar or something you will have readily available at any competition.

## Use a Deep Muscle Relaxation Script

Tension is a huge energy robber. One way to rid yourself of energy-robbing tension is to use a deep-relaxation script. You can either use the one that follows or write your own. Then you can have someone read the script to you or record it on tape and listen to it with headphones.

This script is from *Sports and Exercise Psychology* and was written by Jim Taylor.

- Imagine there are drain plugs on the bottom of your feet. You will undo these plugs and all the tension will drain out of your body and you will become very, very relaxed. Take a long, slow, deep breath.

- Now, undo those plugs. You can feel the tension begin to drain out of your body. Down from the top of your head, past your forehead, your face and your neck; you are becoming more and more relaxed. And the tension drains out of your jaw and down past your neck, and now your face and your neck are warm and relaxed and comfortable. Take a long, slow, deep breath.

- The tension continues to drain out of your upper body, out of your hands and forearms and upper arms and shoulders. Now your hands, arms, and shoulders are warm and relaxed and comfortable. Take a long, slow, deep breath.

- The tension continues to drain out of your upper body, past your chest and upper back, down past your stomach and lower back, and your upper body is becoming more and more relaxed. Now there is no more tension in your upper body. Your entire upper body is warm and relaxed and comfortable. Take a long, slow, deep breath.

- The tension continues to drain out of your body, past your buttocks and down past your thighs and your knees. And your lower body is becoming more and more relaxed. The tension drains out of your calves. Now, there is almost no tension left in your body and the last bit of tension drains past your ankles, the balls of your feet, and your toes. Now there is no more tension left in your body. Your entire body is warm and relaxed and comfortable. Now, replace the plugs so that no tension gets back in. Take a long, slow, deep breath.

If this script does not suit you, change it. Write your own relaxation script below:

If you do not like the idea of using a script then you can just use *progressive relaxation*. Do this by systematically tensing and relaxing each muscle in your body for five seconds. Begin with the muscles in your face, tighten the muscles for five seconds and then relax for five seconds. Now proceed all the way to the muscles in your feet.

Which handler would you rather have?

## Smile!

KATIE GREER said that one of the things she does when at a competition is, *"Smile a lot; there is a lot of truth in if you act it, you will feel it. So smile a lot, and think happy thoughts; recall past glories and how good it felt when we truly clicked as a team. I seek out people that I know will be of good humor and share laughter. Laughing feels good and strengthens nerves. I give myself a pep speech; we all need a coach, so coach yourself if none other exists!"*

So, let us pretend you are at a competition and you are feeling tense and there are four dogs ahead of you. You do not have time to lie on the floor, get your earphones, and relax. You have to go into the ring in just a few minutes. According to Jim Taylor in *Sports and Exercise Psychology*, you can do something *"so basic it is surprising that it is so effective."* You can *smile!* Marketing research has shown that people can hear whether another person on the phone is smiling or not. Well, if other people can hear it over the phone, then how do you think it might affect your dog running along right next to you?

You can also use the smiling technique when you make a handling error on course. Here is how it would work:

1. You make an error.
2. The dog goes off-course.
3. You smile—you feel better. If your dog is very soft, this can also help keep the dog from shutting down. If you are worried that the smile may reinforce your dog, don't. Be happy. After all, the dog only did what you told her to do.

For this technique to work you must hold the smile for at least 60 seconds. So that means even as you are finishing your NQ (non-qualifying) run and crossing the finish line you are smiling. What you will notice is that it is difficult to feel something that is the opposite of your facial expression. In other words, you cannot help but feel happy when you are smiling. Research has shown that smiling changes blood flow through the brain and causes the release of neuro-chemicals that have a relaxing effect (*Sports and Exercise Psychology*, page 94). So keep smiling! It is good for you!

## Top Competitors on Relaxing

Mindy Lytle recommends that you take a second at the start line to feel your heart slow down. Mindy gets to the start line as early as possible so that she can have her moment of calm and then get out there and go for it. During this moment, she literally monitors her heartbeat and waits for it to go up and

Diane Tosh, seen here with her dog Beeg, takes deep breaths at the start line to get more oxygen through her bloodstream and also to help her concentrate on the dog and the run.

PHOTO BY LORI LEWIS.

then come down. When it comes down, she knows she is ready to go and simply waits for the timer to give the signal. All of this happens very quickly, so that Mindy has never caused a delay.

Another technique that Mindy has developed is not listening to the judge when he announces the standard course time. She says that this has helped her stay relaxed and not allowed a course time to make her tense.

DIANE TOSH recommends that if you want to get relaxed before your run and at the start line you need to, *"Number one, not give a hoot about what others think. It is important to learn to focus on you and your dog. I take deep breaths. I think this helps in two ways. I get more oxygen through my bloodstream, enabling me to think better, and it takes my mind off of everything but me and my dog and the run. I concentrate on getting air into the bottom of my lungs and letting it out slowly, kind of like in yoga."* Diane explains how this process helps her relax and how the relaxation helps her get confident.

## Getting Your Dog to Relax

Elicia Calhoun's Australian Shepherd Suni knows how to relax when she's waiting to go into the ring.

PHOTO BY TIEN TRAN.

KATIE GREER recommends that if you have a high-strung dog you might want to, *"Keep them occupied with something else. If they get keyed up watching agility, then stay back from the ring. If they are worried about their surroundings, then keep them occupied so they do not worry. Fun tricks are really wonderful for this."* Another suggestion that Katie has is to let the dog *"blow off some steam."* She suggests doing this by playing games with your dog that involve running back and forth. Katie also points out that more laid-back dogs may prefer *"belly rubs, or going for a walk. Good agility handlers observe their dogs and adapt their practice to what an individual dog needs to bring out the best in him."*

MONICA PERCIVAL says that *"Usually if the handler relaxes the dog will relax; however, each dog is very different. Some dogs relax more if they are out and sitting at ringside with their handlers before a run; other dogs are more relaxed staying in their crates to the last possible second. Some dogs need to burn off some steam with a game of tug or some retrieving; other dogs need to walk around and sniff the show site. A critical part of the game is figuring out what works for YOUR dog."*

Monica Percival's Border Collie Lazer needs some focused retrieving time to burn off a little steam before he goes into the ring. Here he waits not so patiently for the toy to be thrown again! While Lazer will never look as relaxed outside the ring as Suni does, Monica has learned to read the signs that indicate he is no longer overstimulated and is ready to go in the ring and work with her.

PHOTO BY MONICA PERCIVAL.

PATI HATFIELD recommends teaching *"the dog to relax. Massage, favorite toys, and conversation can all be used to communicate to the dog that it is really not so important that the dog needs to stress out. Develop a joyous attitude yourself. Any sports training is just a way for us to play with our dogs. As good handlers/coaches it is up to us to put things in proper perspective for our dogs."*

Pati mentions canine massage as a way to help your dog relax, but if you do not want to massage your dog, simply stroking your dog with long, calming strokes will sooth him.

When you ask STUART MAH, what he recommends to help tense dogs relax, he says, *"Relax the handler. Most dogs do not stress by themselves. They pick it up. If the handler is uptight, so is the dog."*

## Questions to Ask Yourself

| | |
|---|---|
| 1. When you have been relaxed, what has helped to get you relaxed and keep you relaxed? | |
| 2. In situations when you have not been relaxed, what was happening? | |
| 3. At what point did you realize you were not relaxed? | |
| 4. In the future what will you do if a situation, like in the question above, occurs? | |
| 5. What will be your cue that you are tense and not relaxed? (Hint: you can check your breathing or your muscles to get feedback about whether you are tense or not.) | |
| 6. When you realize you are tense, what is your plan? | |
| 7. In the past, what has helped your dog relax while at a trial? | |
| 8. What relaxes your dog at home? How can you use this at trials? | |

## Chapter 8

# No Pressure

*"Meant to be or not .. that is the question!"*

*"You have prepared your dog.*
*Now it is show time.*
*Last minute worrying will change nothing.*
*It is either meant to be or not."*

—Mindy Lytle

Okay, here's the scoop. No one has it together. The pressure is off. You know that handler who you think is the best you have ever seen? She makes mistakes. You know that seminar instructor who danced around the course while demonstrating with her dog? She makes handling mistakes too. So let's take off the pressure-to-be-perfect thumbscrews and have fun!

Katie Greer keeps the pressure from building by focusing what matters most to her—her relationship with her dog and the reasons why that dog is so special to her regardless of agility. Pictured here are Katie and Paul Greer and their canine family.

Katie Greer, says that she deals with pressure by doing the following, *"I do not look over ribbons or prizes; it is not the wanting of these things that will make the run beautiful, it is the desire for a beautiful run. So I do not tempt myself. There will be another day, and it is easier to blow big bucks over worry than to face the challenge, trust the dog to do its part, and run it out. Just the dance itself, do that and everything else will take care of itself. I would much rather have a pretty run that had a bobble or two, than to micromanage and have what I consider to not be a pretty run, whether it was a qualifying run or not."* Notice how Katie deals with pressure by setting a process goal, the "desire for a beautiful run," rather than focusing on a result such as a ribbon, or qualifying.

Katie goes on to say, *"As time draws near to compete, I go through additional physical preparations, which also help to keep me focused upon the task and to ignore any nagging doubts. Each dog is so special in its own way, and I recall each personality and how they fill my life outside of competition. I am also recalling the differences in how each works and how we will do our particular dance. When we step up to the start line I say 'Ready? Let's go get this one!'"* Katie keeps the pressure from building by focusing on her relationship with her dog. After all, that is what really matters. She also ignores thoughts that are not helpful and focuses on what needs to be done.

In addition to the preparations described above, Katie says, *"These are the things that I do just to pacify myself; some of the things I do for the dogs also help me. A favorite is walking around the ring and the grounds after we arrive and have settled in. It is usually when I give myself my little pep talk and let the dogs just be dogs and check the place out. We walk all over the place, they get to lead the way and check out every little thing their hearts desire. It is our quiet time to just be ourselves. Then I'm ready to face the day."*

Several of the competitors interviewed expressed quiet time as an important part of getting ready for competition. Whether this is effective for you will depend on what you find out by experimenting with quiet time. If you use quiet time before a run and find your nerves soaring, then engaging in small talk with others may be a better strategy for you.

Finally, Katie says, *"I watch the competition and cheer for others having a good day, I want to be there, too! Chalk up experience with those not having such a good day and talk with them if they want. I have been there, too. This interaction puts it all into perspective. You win some and you lose some, it's just another day in the park and there's always another one to come."*

## Types of Pressure

There are two basic types of pressure:

- *Intrinsic pressure* is the pressure coming from inside of you that you put on yourself.
- *Extrinsic pressure* is the pressure coming from outside of you (from a family member or an instructor, for example).

If you are on the Agility World Team, for example, you are going to have both intrinsic and extrinsic pressure. World Team competitors get to be on the team because they have put a great deal of pressure on themselves to accomplish what they have. Once they are actually on the team, the desire to do well for their country kicks in. If World Team competitors thought about all of this during their runs, they would never be able to handle their dogs around the course.

## Pressure Creates Stress

The more pressure you feel, the more stressed you will become. Some pressure and a little stress may be good. As discussed earlier, if you are not excited enough you cannot Zone, so some excitement is desirable. However, too much excitement will push you right out of the peak performance Zone and into the stress Zone.

When you are experiencing stress, it is a good idea to be able to measure it. This gives you the opportunity to gather information in terms of how much stress you are experiencing, and become clear about where the stress is coming from.

Dr. Mary Pratt, Stress Management Therapist, has developed a stress ruler that can be used to measure the amount of stress that you are experiencing.

| 1 | 2 | 3 | 4 | 5 | 6 | 7 | 8 | 9 | 10 |
|---|---|---|---|---|---|---|---|---|---|

I can
handle it.

My stress level is
as high as it can be.

Imagine that this ruler is for measuring your personal stress level. Choose the number that shows how you feel right now. Use this to gather information about the stress you are experiencing in competition.

When is the stress the highest and when is it lower? Describe both situations.
*High stress:*

```



```

*Low stress:*

```



```

What competition situations cause you to have the highest numbers?

```



```

In the past, what has helped to reduce your stress?

```



```

The information above is useful for several reasons. First, it enables you to track your improvement, and second, it enables you to expose yourself gradually to more stressful situations, thereby building up your tolerance. Just as you would gradually expose a dog to the competition environment, you can do the same for yourself. This process of gradually getting yourself accustomed to something you previously feared or felt anxious about is called *systematic desensitization*. The funny thing is that while you are desensitizing yourself to what is most stressful to you, you are building your confidence at the same time. By the time you engage in a level 10 stress situation, it will not be nearly as stressful as you had anticipated.

Can you imagine winning two out of three national championships in the same year? Can you imagine the pressure you might be feeling knowing you have won two and wanting to win the third in the same year? Winning the third would mean that you have done what has never been done before in agility history. It would mean winning the Triple Crown of dog agility. Well, it happened. Top competitor Ken Boyd did it. Ken and his dog Becky, a Corgi, won three national championships in the same year.

Ken Boyd says that he felt pressure at the AKC National finals after Becky had won the USDAA and NADAC National finals and he knew he had a chance at the Triple Crown of agility. Instead of allowing this pressure to build and become destructive, he used the energy that the pressure gave him. He spent a great deal of time walking around the facility and removed himself from the ring area. While he was walking, he continuously ran the course with Becky mentally. Ken says that he did not want to relax and, at the same time, did not want to be overly nervous. The walking helped him keep the balance between the two. Ken explains that because of his military involvement he is aware of how fighter pilots and NASA astronauts are trained using flight simulation. He sees his walking the show grounds and mentally rehearsing his course strategy as a way of training himself and using his own version of agility run simulation.

Ken Boyd also advises competitors to *"Stand back and see that this is a game that you play with your dog. Do the best you can and if anything goes wrong, you still walk away from the course winners! No matter what, you did well."* He recommends watching the agility bloopers tape shown at the USDAA 1997 Grand Prix dinner. He explains that besides the tape being hilarious, you can see people goofing up and making mistakes who are all champions now.

## Preventing Panic

One of the things that can occur as the result of pressure is panic. A panicked handler will find herself unable to concentrate or relax. Panic is overarousal. It will definitely knock you out of the Zone.

Prevent panic by

- building your confidence.
- increasing your physical stamina.
- increasing your motivation.
- finding and using the best course memorization technique for you (more on this later).
- physically separating yourself from people who are pressuring you.

It is important not to fear the panic. If you have panicked in competition, it is very important to clear your mind of that experience. Develop a "so what if I panic" attitude. The only power panic has over you is the power you give it. Be patient with yourself—preventing panic is another Masters-level handling skill.

Please note that some people suffer from panic disorder, which is a biochemically based disorder that causes severe panic attacks. If you suspect that you might be suffering from panic disorder, please consult a doctor.

Consider purchasing Suzanne Clothier's self-hypnosis tapes. One tape is for obedience and one is specifically for agility. If you are concerned about panic, these tapes are likely to be helpful to you. The tapes are available by calling Flying Dog Press at 1-800-7 FLY-DOG.

## Techniques for Ridding Yourself of Pressure

So how do World Team competitors do it? How do they rid themselves of pressure? They rid themselves of pressure by using their Zone factors. At the beginning of this book, Stuart Mah describes a Zone run that he had with his dog Shannon. Stuart describes a sense of timelessness. The timelessness happens because Stuart is able to focus so superbly on his dog and his run that he blocks out everything else. Pressure does not exist at that moment because he does not leave any room for it.

Elicia Calhoun recommends *"practicing like you perform, because that way performance will be like practice."* She does this by setting up everything at home like it would be at a trial. Performance then becomes *"expensive practice."*

Taking Elicia's advice means getting some ring gating and making your training area look like a competition ring. You can also always use cones when you are training and make use of entrance and exit gates. You could even go as far as tape recording the noises at an agility show and playing them on a boom box as you run your dog. Anything that helps you get comfortable and familiar with the show atmosphere will be helpful to you. Have a friend judge your practice runs; this will help you become desensitized to being judged.

Pati Hatfield has a different perspective on pressure. She recommends using pressure for an *"edge."* She goes on to say, *"See the pressure as part of the game."* Pati says that she actually likes running courses that make her really nervous, because then she really feels challenged to *"conquer the course."* What Pati is doing is using her nervousness to build confidence. If she can run and *"conquer"* courses that are very difficult, then she can do any course. She is also using pressure to help bump up her arousal to make sure that she will Zone.

Her advice to handlers is to put every competition into perspective—one competition *"is like a leaf in the wind."* She urges handlers to focus on the process, enjoy it, and see the competition as an opportunity to show off your relationship with your dog. Pati explains that the only thing that matters is the relationship with your dog.

Most importantly, Pati says that handlers cannot let the pressure affect them, because they *"have to be out there for the dog."* She draws the analogy of a mother who is caring for a sick child. The mom is worried, but does not let the child see it in order to protect the child. She says you cannot let the dog see your worry or nervousness because of how it will affect the dog. You need to *"be a parent to the dog."*

Following are some ideas for relieving pressure.

### *Accept That Bad Runs Do Not Exist*

There are no bad runs. Let's face it, you do not have control over most things. Bars drop. Kids do eat hot dogs next to the ring, and your dog *does* smell it. Take the pressure off because "stuff happens."

Every "bad" run that you have is actually a good run. It may not be clean but it gives you valuable information about where you and your dog stand. If you had four off-courses, it was a good run because you now know to go home and practice turns and calling your dog off incorrect obstacles.

In addition, if you blow a run early, you can use the rest of the course to practice. This is not training in the ring, which is not allowed; this is trying out a new handling move or working a contact and waiting a few seconds before releasing your dog.

### Minimize Contact with People Who Pressure You

When you try to take your competitiveness to the next level, it is necessary to take a close look at the people who surround you. Please explore the following questions:

Who in your family is supportive of what you are trying to accomplish or of the goals you are setting in terms of agility?

Who in your family is not supportive of what you are trying to accomplish or of the goals you are setting in terms of agility? How has this affected you?

If a non-supportive person has affected you, what can you do to minimize the negative effect on you?

How do your friends react to your agility goals? How has this affected you?

When you are at a competition, what people have a positive effect on you? What people have a negative effect on you?

Evaluate your response to these questions on the basis of who is supportive and who is not. Make an effort to surround yourself primarily with people who are supportive. If you interact with people who are not supportive, do not expect them to change. Do not waste energy trying to get them to be supportive.

Make an effort to minimize contact with people who pressure you when you are already feeling very pressured. If another person is attempting to pressure you, it is your choice to allow that to happen or not. Even if you are unable to limit interaction with the person, you can work on your reaction to what they say. By choosing to control your reaction, you can guard against external pressuring.

### Keeping Busy

While speaking with competitors about their competition experiences, one told me that the *"best run she ever had"* was immediately after accidentally locking herself into a porta-potty. She said that she was nervous about the competition and wanted to empty her bladder one more time. When she tried to exit the porta-potty, she realized that she was locked in and unable to get out. In a frantic panic, she kicked and slammed at the door and finally after a few minutes she was freed. At this point there was no more time to warm up or to get nervous. She only had time to grab her dog and run into the ring. The result was the best run she ever had.

What the porta-potty story teaches us is that keeping busy until it is your turn to go can be a good strategy in preventing the pressure from building or keeping the show nerves from latching on.

Show nerves latch on when you raise your expectations about what should happen in the ring.

### Be Your Own Best Friend

Most of us are not our own best friends. We are more like our own worst critics. Just monitor what you say to yourself after you have made a handling mistake in the ring. What we say to ourselves, and how we care for ourselves physically are very important in preventing Zone-destructive pressure.

When competing, focus on getting the following physical needs met:

- Thirst (avoid sugary beverages and alcohol).
- Hunger (eat nutritious food).
- Get plenty of sleep (this can be a challenge in a noisy motel) and take naps if necessary.
- Keep your body temperature at a comfortable level.

When your physical needs are met, you are significantly increasing the chances of a Zone performance. The cool thing about the physical needs pre-

BUD HOUSTON suggests that one way of ridding yourself of pressure is by ridding yourself of expectations in terms of your handling. *"The higher your expectations about how you will do, the more disappointed you will be in yourself. Expectations and the pressure they create are contrary to what you really want to be at the competition."*

As JULIE DANIELS puts it, *"I have also learned, the hard way, what and when to eat and drink during big competitions. This is an individual thing which takes some experimentation."*

Julie Daniels reminds us that finding the right routine for ourselves in terms of what to eat and drink during big competitions is just as important as finding out the right routine for our dogs. Here Julie is pictured with her dogs Arrow, Jessy, and Spring.

viously listed is that most of them are easily controlled. It is easy to carry water with you and have access to it at all times. You already do that for your dog. It is easy to carry healthy snack food with you to the trial. You would never leave home without your dog's nutritious food. It is amazing how pressured a competitor can feel as the result of not having her physical needs met. When the competitor stops to take the time to eat and drink, most of the pressure dissipates.

Our physical needs and our ability to perform at a peak level are subject to cycles. There are times of the day where you will automatically perform better because of this cycle. The same is true of dogs. A puppy is playing one second and crashed out on the floor the next. Dogs go through periods of rest and activity every day. Morning people recognize that their daily cycle dictates that they are at their peak in the morning. If you are interested in reading about these daily cycles, there is a book called *The 20-Minute Break* by Dr. Ernest Rossi that discusses these cycles in detail. Rossi's main premise is that if you take a 20-minute break before expecting peak performance, your performance will be better than if you had not taken the break. Rossi describes the breaks as rest periods that do not involve talking or interaction of any kind. After a 20-minute break the benefits will last up to 90 to 120 minutes, at which point another 20-minute break is recommended.

The longer you deny yourself rest, the longer a period of rest will be required to balance you out again. If, for example, you had no sleep during the night and have no rest during the day, you are greatly reducing the odds of having a Zone performance. When you understand your daily cycles of hunger, thirst, and rest, you can use them to help you get and stay in your Zone.

No research has been done on the cycles of rest and activity of dogs; however, it seems that the same rules would apply. This means that you evaluate whether your dog is in an activity or rest period and then take the necessary steps to get your dog in the Zone. If your dog seems a little tired, hose her down to help her get the extra energy she needs to get into her Zone. If your dog seems very active, calm her with massage or tire her out with playing ball so that she becomes a little less aroused and is able to perform in her Zone.

Another aspect of being your own best friend is carefully monitoring your self-talk. Have you ever listened to the merciless verbal abuse we subject ourselves to? For instance, if we are running late we call ourselves idiots. Or if we make a mistake in competition we beat ourselves up with, "I should have…" or "I ought to…" This negative self-talk is extremely counter-productive in helping us reach and stay in the Zone. Just as your dog cues off your body language, your brain cues off your thoughts. Thinking precedes feeling and doing, so when you think that you are stupid for calling the obstacle late, you are placing the thought of calling late in your mind. That will certainly add pressure and may bump you out of the Zone. You are also harming your confidence by calling yourself "stupid." When it comes to negative self-talk there is one rule: Just *don't* do it!

### Use Positive Self-Talk to Soothe Show Nerve Pressure

When you feel the nervousness coming on, reason with yourself that it is perfectly okay for you to feel nervous and that nervousness is cool. The nervousness means that you are ready and at your peak. Tell yourself anything you want about the butterflies in your belly, but make sure it is positive. If what you are telling yourself soothes your nerves, then do more of it. If you feel a knot when you tell yourself something, change it. This is a process, so be patient and keep track of what works. Remember that distraction can be a great way to forget about nerves or pressure.

## Emotions That Create Pressure

JANE SIMMONS-MOAKE describes this very dynamic. When she experienced pressure at the 1996 World Championships her reaction was excitement, not stress. She describes the situation like this, *"It was the last course of the weekend and I was the last of the U.S. team members to run. I knew that if I did well our team would be in very good shape in the standings. Although the pressure was on, I was pleasantly surprised to find myself experiencing not nerves, but exhilaration. I believe this feeling of focused, positive excitement helped me reach the Zone in this final, culminating run."*

If you do not want to experience any pressure while competing, you must get yourself to a place where you do *not* care about the outcome of your performance. When you do not care about the outcome of the run, you will experience no pressure. This is a Masters-level Zone skill and takes a while to develop. Using the "do not care" attitude to take off pressure will only work if you *do* care about something simple like making your dog smile while running in the ring. Total apathy about a run means your arousal will be too low and no Zoning will occur.

A note here regarding advanced competitors. Highly competitive, world-class competitors may want to experience some pressure if it historically has helped them increase arousal when they have not been excited enough. For some seasoned competitors it may be helpful to allow pressure to build to help increase arousal and give them the extra push they need to get into their peak performance Zone. Zoning is a balancing act of under and overarousal.

## How Pressure Affects Our Four-Legged Friends

Some dogs are very sensitive to pressure. As handlers, it is our responsibility to try to maintain an environment that keeps these dogs from feeling pressure. Pressure-sensitive dogs will shut down, run out of the ring, start stress sniffing, or simply stare at you. Regardless of how the dog communicates her discomfort, you must learn how to recognize it and prevent it from happening.

Does your dog perform wonderfully at home and at other familiar locations, but when you enter her in a competition her training falls apart? You might have a pressure-sensitive dog.

Prevent pressuring your dog by

- being overprepared for your run.

- making sure you are confident in your handling and the level at which you are competing.

- not allowing any negative thoughts to enter your mind.

- making sure that your focus is where it needs to be.

- using visualization and relaxation to help you behave as if competition were practice.

## Testing Your Students' Reaction to Pressure

If you teach an agility class, surprise your students with a pop quiz. Bud Houston suggested this idea in *Clean Run* magazine a few years back. Put on a stern face and announce that each student will run a course that you will time and grade. Tell them anything else that you think will crank up the pressure; maybe you want to give them a speech about how you expect them to do well, and how disappointed you will be if one of them does not make time and run clean. Anything you can say to really get your students to squirm with pressure is good.

Proceed to follow up on your threat and begin tightening the thumbscrews. Have each student run a course that you both time and grade. Make a big deal about this. But instead of actually grading the students on their runs, you will be taking notes on how they are reacting to the artificial pressure you created. Make sure to look serious and not smile. Use the remainder of the class to focus on the following:

1. The reaction of each student.
2. The quality of each student's run in light of the artificial pressure.
3. The reaction of the dog to the student being pressured.
4. What type of thoughts the student had and how they might be replaced with more positive and constructive thoughts.
5. Creating an action plan for what to do when a real-life pressure situation occurs.

Please note that it is best *not* to repeat this exercise. Once you have gained the information about your students' reactions, it is not necessary to put your students through this stress again.

## Questions to Ask Yourself

| | |
|---|---|
| 1. What have been the competitive situations that have been most pressuring to you? | |
| 2. When you have felt pressured at a competition and were able to rid yourself of *some* or all of the pressure, how did you accomplish this? | |
| 3. How has your dog been affected by you feeling pressured? | |
| 4. How can you best support your dog when you are feeling pressured? | |

# Chapter 9

# Energizing

*"Think: I own this course. Confidence is energizing!"*

—BUD HOUSTON

*B*eing underaroused and needing energizing is usually what happens to long-time agility competitors who no longer find themselves challenged by "regular competitions." If you are a fairly new competitor, this chapter may be less helpful to you.

Imagine you wake up the morning of a competition with only four hours of sleep. You had set your alarm for as late as possible to squeeze out precious minutes of extra sleep, and now you go tearing downstairs, grab your dog, and head out the door. Halfway to the show grounds you realize you have forgotten your dog food and packed no lunch for yourself. You get to the show grounds and do not have time to pitch your tent and have to ask a friend to hold your dog while you run to join the other competitors who have already been walking the course. You are tired and frustrated and super low on energy. Now what? Energize!

> KATIE GREER says that, *"When I'm not feeling up to things, the first thing I do is get my dog out and just go for a walk. My partner needs a leader who is ready to lead. We explore the site and I regroup. Chances are I was feeling overloaded from all the excitement, people, and goings-on, and just needed a bit of time to myself. I frequently find that I need a break from all the activity that surrounds agility trials, otherwise it can all be quite overwhelming to me."*

Taking a quiet walk by yourself after being rushed or running late can be very relaxing. Even if it is only for a few minutes, a short walk can do wonders in getting yourself calmed and getting your energy back.

> During the walk KATIE says, *"I watch my dog enjoying the finer things in life, sniffing the smells, listening to the sounds, and watching the sights. I find myself drifting into the world they are experiencing, and life is good again. This is the same thing I do to calm my nerves when first arriving at the show site. It seems to work both ways, it calms me and also rejuvenates me, and the end result is that I feel prepared to enter the ring when it's time."*

## Pump Yourself Up

Use energizing when you need to pump yourself up. Take another look at the Zone graph on the left. Just as the graph demonstrates, if you are not pumped up enough, your performance suffers.

If you notice that you are not excited enough, you can experiment with listening to music that pumps you up before going in the ring. How would the music of "Rocky" or "Chariots of Fire" affect you? Experiment with this ahead of time, so that when you need energizing you can do what works best. You can also select an energizing phrase and repeat it to yourself.

Create a list of the things that are energizing to you.

Listening to

Reading

Talking with

Napping for (always set an alarm clock)

Spending time with

Talking about

Analyzing

Planning

Brainstorming about

Laughing about

When competing, around _____ o'clock I tend to get tired. In case I ever need to run my dog at that time, I will help myself be energetic by

## Use a Certain Word to Trigger an Energizing Response

Just like when you use a keyword to trigger a relaxation response, you can use a keyword to trigger energizing. Experiment with the following words or phrases and see which one has an energizing effect on you:

- Go for it!
- I own this course! (Bud Houston)
- Charge!
- Positive!
- Fun!
- This course is not going to get us out! (Marq Cheek)

The most important thing about energizing is to learn when you need to use it. Learning to recognize when you need firing up is another mental handling skill. Whether you need to energize yourself or not is very subjective. Some people will need to use their energizing tool frequently, while others never need one.

In the past, I have needed to be energized when

*Example:* When I volunteered to help run the show in addition to competing with my own dog.

NANCY GYES says that she is always feeling energized before a run: *"Needing to get pumped up at a show rarely happens. If I feel tired, I have a cup of coffee. The start line winds me up if that does not work."*

JANE SIMMONS-MOAKE explains that she tries to, *"Walk around rather than sit, then do some stretches. Often I will drink a Diet Coke or some caffeinated beverage. The most energizing thing I do, however, is taking my dog out of her crate. She is always bouncy and ready to go. Her enthusiasm is contagious. By the time we are through warming up we are both psyched and ready to go!"*

PATI HATFIELD has an entirely different approach to energizing. When asked what she does when an energy low strikes she replied, *"I do not have any right to be tired and drained before a run. It is my responsibility to be what my dog needs me to be. How can I ask less of myself than I do of my dog?"* Pati adds, *"Prior to a run, I can become totally focused and centered on my dog regardless of how I might be feeling."*

As with all the Zone strategies, you will need to experiment and find the proper energizing technique that works for you.

Many top competitors, such as Nancy Gyes (seen here with her Border Collie Scud), find that they don't need to do anything extra to get energized at a show. Walking up to the start line is enough!

## Questions to Ask Yourself

| | |
|---|---|
| 1. In the past, when you have needed to energize yourself, what has been helpful in accomplishing that? | |
| 2. What has not been helpful? How can these things be eliminated or minimized? | |
| 3. What helps your dog get energized? | |

**Chapter 10**

# *Overlearning*

*Overlearning is muscle memory for your brain.*

Overlearning occurs when you have practiced something so much that it becomes like a reflex. Athletes refer to overlearning as *body memory* or *muscle memory*. Muscle memory happens when you have rehearsed and practiced so much that you are able to do the movement unconsciously. Overlearning has the wonderful side effect of helping us feel very confident, because the behavior has become second nature. You can use overlearning for anything, including agility. Use overlearning in agility so that all the handling moves you will ever want to make are completely smooth and require no thought on your part. All of the strategies for getting and staying in the Zone can be overlearned.

## Four Levels of Competence

According to Dr. Robert Singer of the University of Florida Sports Psychology Department, "*Practicing and training should result in being able to do the movement required by your sport with subconscious attention.*" This means overlearning has taken place.

One way to track this is by using the commonly known four levels of competence:

1. The first level is when you are *subconsciously incompetent.* This is the point where you do not know much about agility so you do not know that you have no clue how to handle a dog around an agility course. You are unaware of your incompetence.

2. The second level is when you are *consciously incompetent.* This means you are now aware of agility and handling skills and are aware that your handling skills need improvement.

3. The third level of competence is when you are *consciously competent.* This means you are now guiding your dog around a course and are very conscious of your movements and when you are calling obstacles.

4. The final level is the one that is most important in terms of Zoning. When you are *subconsciously competent*, the learning process has reached its peak. Now you are guiding your dog around a course effortlessly and, seemingly to you, without any significant effort. You are dancing courses with your dog.

Overlearning is *subconscious competence*. When you have overlearned something, you feel like the skill has become part of you. Our dogs acquire this skill too. For instance, when a dog learns the rhythm of the weave poles, and consistently executes them flawlessly, that dog is subconsciously competent at weaving.

## Repetition and Learning

MARQ CHEEK recommends, *"Judging and watching others is one of the best ways of learning. For newcomers, I highly recommend that they get to the trials early and make a point of watching the best handlers in their area. All too often, I see the beginners arrive late and hover around the novice ring. There is a vast wealth of knowledge and experience usually competing just one ring away... Get there!"*

As dog trainers we are aware that dogs require a high degree of repetition to have truly learned a new behavior. We are also aware of the fact that to generalize to all situations, the new behavior must be learned in a variety of settings. While humans are much more mentally sophisticated than dogs, the same principles still apply.

Some statistics say that a person requires 200 repetitions to learn. If this is accurate, then you require 200 front crosses to internalize that handling maneuver. But wait, those crosses were all from the left to the right, so you have to do 200 more from the right to the left. Then you have to do the same thing for rear crosses, advanced hand signals, or commands like "Get out." You are not just training your dog here. If you want to Zone, you have to repeatedly train your movements and the timing of your commands just as you would repeatedly train your dog.

As humans, we have the tremendous advantage of being able to learn by mimicry. Dogs do not learn by imitating other dogs, but we can use this technique to assist us in overlearning. By watching advanced competitors you can begin the process of being unconsciously competent at handling your dog.

Monica Percival says that *"agility is about being able to react to your dog in a fraction of a second when things don't go exactly as planned."* It is impossible to do two things at the same time. You cannot focus on your handling moves and at the same time watch your dog for an unexpected step so that you can react to it. By overlearning your handling moves, you free yourself up to react to what your dog is doing in the ring and manage performance.

With the variety of dogs she has worked in agility, Monica Percival has learned that a key element in succeeding in the sport is learning how to constantly react to the dog you are running. Handling fundamentals and remembering the course need to be second-nature so that they come to you almost automatically and you can completely focus on the dog performing each obstacle.

PHOTO BY ANNA JONSSON.

## Questions to Ask Yourself

| | |
|---|---|
| 1. What has been an effective method for you to practice your handling and mental skills until you have overlearned them? | |
| 2. What has prevented you from overlearning and how can you avoid this? | |
| 3. Has your dog overlearned the skills required of him at your current level of competition? If not, what skills need to be overlearned? | |
| 4. What will you do to help your dog overlearn the skills listed above? | |

## Chapter 11

# *Competition*

*"We absolutely have a blast out there.
We do not take ourselves seriously. There is no ego involved.
We are not afraid to embarrass ourselves.
We have no expectations."*

—KEN BOYD ON THE KEY TO HIS AND BECKY'S SUCCESS

## Prepare a Pre-Competition Ritual

If you watch professional athletes, you will notice that they always do certain things exactly the same way before they compete. If you watch the top agility competitors before they go in the ring, you will notice that they always repeat certain behaviors. What you are observing is a *pre-competition ritual.* Competitors use these rituals to get grounded, to get ready, to get to their starting point. They may not even be aware that they are doing it. Pre-competition rituals can be very simple things like how they warm up the dog or how they take off the dog's leash and collar.

If you get nervous before entering the ring, prepare a ritual that will help calm and relax you. If you are not pumped up enough, prepare a ritual that helps get you energized. Do *not* experiment with this at a show. This is something you practice first. Then you use only the rituals that have proven effective. Consider that you probably already have some pre-competition rituals and evaluate how they are working for you.

Use the same strategy for your dog. If she needs to be pumped up before going in the ring, prepare a ritual that will help her get excited. If your dog needs to be calmed or soothed, use the Tellington-Touch to assist her in relaxing. *T-Touch* is the technique of massaging your dog with little circular movements. Other pre-competition rituals can include throwing a toy, stretching, repeating certain phrases to the dog, or doing certain tricks to help the dog get focused. Remember that dogs can see our thoughts in our body language, so keep everything positive and have fun!

When preparing a pre-competition ritual for you or your dog, Dr. Singer of the University of Florida Sports Psychology Department says it is important to consider the following:

- **The individual person and dog involved.** Do you need calming or energizing? What gets your dog into the Zone?
- **The activity in which the dog and handler team is about to participate.** What is the level of competition and the nature of competition? Is it a Gamblers course or a Standard course that requires you and the dog to work close together?
- **Stress management.** Make sure the pre-competition ritual reduces stress.

A pre-competition ritual can be *macro* or *micro*. What this means is that some pre-competition rituals begin days before the actual competition (macro) and that other rituals are performed right before the actual competition (micro). When evaluating what rituals work best for you, be sure to evaluate both macro and micro.

My macro pre-competition ritual is

```



```

My micro pre-competition rituals are

```



```

One of the concerns of competitors can be that there is so much to do during the warm-up period, how will they have time to do all the things that will make a Zone run happen?

**Warm-Up Checklist**

- ❑ Warm up yourself and stretch.
- ❑ Warm up your dog and stretch.
- ❑ Massage your dog.
- ❑ Implement pre-competition ritual.
- ❑ Review course one last time.
- ❑ Perform any other tasks that might be helpful to the warming-up process.

No matter how you decide to warm up, Pati Hatfield encourages you to start early. Pati says, *"The real point is that I do not want to get stressed over a warm-up jump. Why put myself in that position before I run my dog?"* Get to the jump early and you will have plenty of time for the rest of your pre-competition ritual.

This seems like a lot to do in the few minutes before you go in to compete; however, this list gets a lot shorter when you start combining tasks and incorporating them into your pre-competition ritual.

For example, you could make all of the warm-up checklist part of your pre-competition ritual. You massage your dog to warm her up. While you are doing that, you work on your focus. Next, you head for the warm-up jump and stretch yourself and your dog while you are waiting for your turn. Then you use your time at the warm-up jump to practice some of the challenging movements that will be required. Finally, connect with your dog by making her "spin" and "twist" and "back" and "front." You are done and ready to Zone.

List all of the tasks that you would like to complete before entering the ring. Please list them in order of priority, beginning with the most important task. Do this so that if your list gets too long you can choose the top tasks only.

1.

2.

3.

4.

5.

6.

7.

8.

9.

10.

Now combine the tasks to create your own pre-competition ritual. Begin your warm-up with the most important tasks.

## Top Competitors and Their Pre-Competition Rituals

Top competitor Pati Hatfield repeats the same pre-competition ritual at every show. The first thing is to let Lilly sniff and go to the bathroom and "be a dog." While Lilly does this, Pati stretches. Next Pati and Lilly begin playing games. Pati gradually increases the intensity of these games as both she and Lilly warm up their muscles. Then Pati moves on to doing some fast turns with her dog. She then returns to her van to put away the toy. Finally, Pati proceeds to the practice jump to warm up for jumping.

After the practice jump Pati usually has five to six competitors ahead of her. Now she focuses Lilly on performing tricks. Pati says that it is okay for people to talk with her during this process, but that she makes sure that Lilly *"never stops watching me."* Pati makes sure that the connection with her dog is not broken until after she is done with her run.

KEN BOYD describes his pre-competition ritual like this: *"We like to do a flyball start. I set Becky at the start line and hold her back like you would for a restrained recall. This really revs her up. I tell her 'ready-set-go' and she is pulling to break free at the same time and never waits for me to say go. The cheating is part of the game. If I need to lead out, I do the same thing just with the words 'ready-set-go.' The whole time I am daring her to go."*

NANCY GYES says, *"I try to put my energies into warming up my dog properly, finding tough elements of the course that I can somehow practice at the warm-up jump, or with some kind of an exercise with my dog."*

MARQ CHEEK uses visualization in his pre-competition ritual. Marq explains, *"If you have ever watched lugers in the Olympics, you will see them going over the course with their eyes closed and they move their bodies as they go through the imaginary turns on their way down the imaginary course. I decided if I could do the course with my eyes closed, then I would know the course and know the moves I needed to perform. The more I practiced this imagery, the more real it became. I could see the obstacles and their paint schemes, I could see the lump of weed where I wanted to pivot, I could see myself switching hands and feel myself conducting a critical move like the reverse flow pivot at just the right time."*

Please note that a pre-competition ritual can center around whatever is most important for you to Zone; for Marq, it is knowing the course and what his body movements will be on the course.

Linda Mecklenburg, seen here at the 1996 USDAA National Championships with her Border Collie Nifty, has a low-key pre-competition ritual that has been very successful for her. The important thing is to find what works for you.

LINDA MECKLENBURG describes her pre-competition ritual like this: *"When I am in the on-deck area, I once again review the course in my mind while looking out onto the field. If it is a big competition, I am usually now nervous. I perform a bit better with some tension though, so I do not let it bother me. The extra adrenaline gives me the edge that helps me react more quickly and keep up with my fast dogs. I do take a nice deep breath the last thing as I leave my dog at the start line."*

Linda explains, *"My warm-ups with my dog are casual. Just a few jumps to let them know they are about to go to work is all they need. They get bored with more. I will watch a few runs to be sure there is not a problem area I did not anticipate."* This low-key approach to her pre-competition rituals has been very successful for Linda.

SUSAN GARRETT says that each of her dogs requires a different pre-competition ritual. *"For the dogs' warm-up you have to know your dogs and what they need to help prepare them to run fast but at the same time always listen to you. Of course all of this begins with a good solid foundation of motivational training at home. The dog is not going to mysteriously become brilliant on the course if you have not put in the hours at home first.*

*Each of my dogs has a different warm-up based on what they need. I like to get everyone physically ready with running and stretching, but mentally they are all different. Often a combination of motivation and obedience works. With Shelby, I will 'hype' her more than the others. She is ten years old and is very reliable on equipment. She still runs fast and loves the games so she is very straightforward to handle compared to the other dogs. At the opposite end of the warm-up scale is Twister. She comes self-hyped about agility so her warm-up is far more subdued. If I thought burning incense while humming softly would help Twister, I might try that! I wish I could tell you that every time I did 'X' we had a 'Zoned run.' If it were that easy, you would see me 'Xing' all over the place. Unfortunately, agility is not that simple and dogs are not that predictable. The last thing I will do while I am standing at ringside waiting to go in the ring is visualize, in my mind, my dog and I running the course. It will be a clear picture with that particular dog that I am about to enter the ring with. I will whisper my cues, bend my body, and complete a clean run over and over again in my mind's eye and then I will step up to the start line."*

As you can see from the different descriptions above, pre-competition rituals are very individual. Each competitor will need to find the rituals that work best for him. Repeat what works; eliminate what does not.

## Monitoring Your Zone Factors in Competition

It's show time! The following are reminders of all the Zone factors that have been discussed previously. Think about each of these categories and how they can help you Zone in competition. By monitoring your Zone factors, you can make adjustments as necessary.

### Result-Oriented Goals

Be aware of your goals for each specific run. Goals that can be very destructive have this very sneaky way of smuggling themselves into competition. When this happens, the result is usually not a Zone run. Be aware of result-oriented goals and their stealth abilities and keep your radar in overdrive. Do this by mentally fixating on your process goals (such as fun, making your dog smile, or trying out a new handling move) and not allowing any mental room for destructive goals.

### Motivation and Confidence

How is your motivation? Are you feeling challenged? Make sure to get a last-minute reading of your level of motivation at each competition so that you can make adjustments.

How is your confidence? Are you overconfident? Are you lacking confidence? Now is the time to gather the information quickly and then take the necessary steps to make adjustments. If you are too confident, find some additional challenges in the course or pretend that the standard course time is 10 seconds less than announced by the judge. If you do not feel confident enough, *lower* your expectations.

### Your Thoughts

Are you thinking fun thoughts? For most of us, agility is a hobby. Remember that you engage in a hobby for fun. Even if you are in agility professionally, the reason you decided to do agility full time was because it was fun. Guarding against negative thoughts while competing is very important.

### Focus

If you tend to have problems focusing in competition, take your time; do not rush yourself. Walk the course until you are whistled off. Give yourself plenty of time to warm up. Make sure your confidence is where it needs to be and run your course with only your "focus word" in mind.

### Visualization

Use only the visualization techniques you have practiced. Last-minute visualization can center around course memorization, your handling movements, and where your dog will be and how she will be running the course. Another option is to use visualization to help you relax or to energize if you need to.

### Relaxing

Monitor your body for tension and check in to see how you are breathing. If you are tense, implement your proven relaxation technique as soon as possible. Getting to that point of balance between relaxation and tension while at a competition is an advanced skill and will take time, so be patient.

### Pressure

If you have determined that pressure is not helpful in getting you to Zone, you will want to work on eliminating your thoughts and behaviors that create pressure. Many of the skills overlap to create a Zone run, so if pressure is the problem, look at your confidence and evaluate your body for tension.

### Energizing

In order to Zone, your energy must be high. High energy means good reaction times. Agility is all about timing and reaction. Use the information that you have gathered in the Energizing chapter to help you get the energy you need to have a Zone run. Keep in mind that your dog's arousal state must also be at the proper level.

### Overlearning

The Overlearning chapter discussed the importance of repeating handling movements until you are subconsciously competent in executing them. Ideally, all the handling moves that you are planning during your run are movements that you could make in your sleep. If not, lower your expectations in regard to your performance.

## Your Dog at a Competition

Pati Hatfield recommends that competitors focus on their dogs. Before each competition, Pati makes sure that Lilly is where she needs to be. Pati emphasizes the importance of "reading" your dogs and knowing where they are so that you can adjust accordingly. She explains that for her this process begins days before a competition and may mean giving Lilly a light day if she seems tired. When actually at the competition, Pati sacrifices socializing and going to dinner with other competitors so that she can be with Lilly and help her rest. Pati explains that it is important to help Lilly rest, because if she does not help her, Lilly is "never still" on her own.

MARQ CHEEK describes what he does with his dog prior to competition like this: *"On the day of competition, I try to get to the site an hour early, and I try to make sure my dog has eaten, something like oatmeal, at least one and a half hours before competing. We will walk at the show site to get smelling and pottying out of the way. He then is penned and will come out about 20 dogs before his run for loosening up and chasing his favorite basketball or hula-hoop. I take him to the practice jump with a few treats to get him jazzed up to jump. We practice a figure eight on the practice jump and some straight, fast, run-ahead approaches. I then take him back for a treat at his crating area. When it is nearing our turn, I either take a ball or some treats."*

Marq continues to say, *"If it is a Gamble and I want him to work at a distance, I usually take a ball and throw it out ahead of him. I try to wind him up to the point that he is almost naughty and will perform obstacles at further distances as he looks away from me. Prior to a trappy course, a busy jumpers course, or before a tricky snooker course, I will take some treats and work with and near the practice jump. I perform some handling maneuvers that I plan on using on the course and my dog has to come in to me and watch me to get treats. I will leave the ball or treats somewhere in the vicinity, but not right next to the ring. When we are done with the run, I will ask him if he wants a 'treat' or 'Where is the ball, you Champion?'*

*If you keep it fun for your dog, he will perform for you better and better each time. If you make a mistake, and they happen to us all, you need to disguise your disappointment and let your teammate think he did wonderfully. If I make a mistake on the course that sends him past a jump or forces him into an incorrect weave entry, I almost never fix it while on the course. If we have NQ'd, then there is no sense trying to repair the damage on the spot. I never want my dog to think he has made a mistake; being in the ring during competition should be fun for the dog."*

## Keeping Competition Fun

Competitors who have been playing the agility trial game for a while can get weary of all the traveling, packing, and organizing involved. Consider the following to keep competition fun:

- Keep a shelf in your garage specifically for agility trial equipment. This way you can unload and load your vehicle in minutes.
- Maintain a list of the most important items that you need to pack. Laminate it and hang it off the "agility shelf" for that last-minute check before you pull out of the garage.
- Purchase a dolly to help transport bulky or heavy items at the show.
- Invest in a lightweight tent rather than a heavy one.
- Invest in a lightweight, mesh crate. They are much easier to transport and set up.

Whatever idea you have that makes the showing process simpler and easy is one worth implementing. Do not underestimate how draining minor annoyances can be. Several small annoyances can add up and kick you right out of your Zone.

## Your First Competition

The following are some suggestions to keep in mind if you are going to your first competition:

- **Read the rulebook of the organization you are showing under.** Make sure you know exactly what type of performance is required to earn a clean run.
- **Arrive early.** Nothing can cause nerves to flare up like being late to your first competition.
- **Plan ahead.** Bring lawn chairs, a canopy for shade, food, and drinks. Competitors need to be prepared to spend a lot of time waiting.
- **Watch as many of the advanced competitors as you can.** A great way to learn is by watching seasoned competitors perform advanced handling techniques.
- **Make sure that you and your dog are overprepared for competition.** If you are competing in AKC Novice, you should be able to successfully run AKC Open courses in practice. Likewise if you are showing USDAA Starters, then you want to be running USDAA Advanced in practice sessions.
- **Find an experienced travel partner with whom you can attend the show.** By traveling with a seasoned competitor you will have someone available to answer questions, and they can give you valuable hints on your handling strategy.

- **Keep in mind that your dog will be exposed to many different dogs.** Not all of these dogs may feel like socializing. Ask the handler if it is okay before allowing your dog to sniff and say "hi" to another dog. Work to prevent distracting other competitors while they are walking the course, warming their dogs up, or standing in line to go into the ring.

- **Bring several toys and treats and plenty of food and water for your dog.** Your dog is new to competing too, and she may have some special needs as a result. Generally, dogs do not nap as much at a competition as they do at home, so do what you can to help your dog rest.

- **Keep your dog quiet.** Barking is stressful to both dogs and handlers. Realistically, your dog will bark at a competition. Many dogs bark excitedly during their run or when other dogs come close to their crates or X-pens. Keep treats handy to reward your dog for being quiet.

- **Smile!** You have just started competing in one of the most enjoyable forms of dog sport. Get ready to have a blast!

## Questions to Ask Yourself

| | |
|---|---|
| 1. What are the three most helpful things for you to focus on when you are competing? | |
| 2. In the past what has *not* worked for you when you are competing? | |
| 3. What can you change as the result of knowing what has not worked for you? | |

**Chapter 12**

# Walking the Course and Course Memorization

*"May the course be with you."*

—Marq Cheek

There are many ways to memorize a course. You can memorize each obstacle, you can memorize segments, you can backchain the sequence (that is, begin by memorizing the last obstacle and work backward to the first), or you can use the color of obstacles to help you memorize complicated Jumpers courses. The key to success when memorizing courses is practice and experience. The more you practice memorizing courses, the better you will get at it. Your memory is like a muscle, so practice will make it strong.

When you are memorizing a course, you are actually learning a sequence of obstacles or a pattern (depending on your memorization style). One thing that can be helpful is knowing your learning style. There are three kinds of learning styles:

- Visual

- Auditory

- Kinesthetic

Learning style researchers say that 70% of us are visual learners. So, the odds are that you are a visual learner, but it is really important to try out all three learning styles before deciding which one works best for you.

If you are a *visual learner,* you learn by seeing. This is someone who has to take notes about everything she is learning. This person is likely to draw charts and organize information by drawing in the margin. Glancing at these notes will help the visual learner recall what was said. The visual learner does this so that she can *see* what the person is saying. Visual learners enjoy using visualization.

The *auditory learner* learns by hearing. This is someone who can sit in class and recall everything said without taking any notes. The auditory learner will most likely focus on what obstacle to call when. It may be helpful to the auditory learner to make a list of exactly what she will say to her dog for the entire run, and then spend time repeating the list of commands aloud.

Finally, *kinesthetic learners* learn by doing. Kinesthetic learners want to do the activity, not hear about it, or even see how it is done. Kinesthetic learners can benefit from listening to music while walking the course; this can help them create a dance out of their handling movements and thereby enhance memorization. Kinesthetic handlers prefer memorizing movement.

Katie Greer describes a kinesthetic learning style when she explains that she memorizes the course according to how it feels—where her body needs to be and at what point she will make what movement. All of Katie's description of memorizing the course is very physical: *"There are X number of obstacles, just do each one, each after the other. I visualize the course, rotate in place and feel the position I will need to be in and the motion I will need to make to direct the dog, so that I feel that I 'remember' the course."* Notice how Katie uses the word "feel" and her emphasis on body position and the "motion" she will need to make. She then concludes that this process helps her remember the course. Katie is memorizing the motions. This is the kinesthetic learning style.

An example of a competitor who uses two learning styles is Ken Boyd. Ken uses both visual and kinesthetic learning styles to memorize courses. He uses visualization to memorize his handling movements for the course (visual learning). His goal for the visualization exercise is to make the movements automatic (kinesthetic learning). Ken explains that when the handling movements are automatic it gives him time to deal with the unexpected. This is tremendously powerful, since it enables him to make minor corrections before an error actually occurs. Ken combines visual and kinesthetic learning to create a powerful combination that enables him to memorize his body movements so well that he can adapt to any unexpected movement his dog might offer.

If you are memorizing a course, you can draw a pattern of the dog's path and your path and see the course (visual), or you can verbalize all your commands and thereby "hear" the course (auditory). And you can actually run the course in the walk-through, thereby programming the motions that will be needed for you to successfully steer your dog (kinesthetic). It is recommended that you try all of the learning styles listed. Once you are confident in terms of memorizing the course you can experiment with which learning style, or combination of learning styles, works best for you.

## Top Competitors on Course Memorization

JULIE DANIELS is another visual learner. She has developed a visualization technique that assists her in memorizing courses. Julie describes the visualization she uses like this: *"I know the course as well as if I had designed it. I can picture it in whole or in segments as if I had wide-angle and zoom capability. My internal camera films the course from above, looking down and showing me and my dog nailing the sequences. That helps me feel the big picture of my handling plan. So before we go into the ring I am comfortable and familiar with the course."* Julie uses the course memorization process to learn the course and to build her confidence. It is common to see course memorization and confidence go hand in hand, since one boosts the other.

LINDA MECKLENBURG uses visualization to mentally rehearse her course memorization. *"Once the walk-through is over, I like to have a few moments to myself where I visualize the course in my mind. I start at the first obstacle and then imagine each command I will give, and where my dog will be, and I envision the course. The more important the competition, the more I focus in this manner. I want to know the course to the extent that I can visualize the actual obstacles. I should be able to say what color the obstacles are, whether or not the jumps are wingless or winged, single or double (or triple), where they are in relation to the ring edge, etc. If I cannot review the entire course in my mind without looking back onto the field, I do not know it well enough."*

Linda describes a process of memorizing and then testing that memorization by getting detail, such as type of jump or color, from what you are visualizing. If Linda is unable to get the details in her visualization, she knows that she has not spent enough time memorizing and visualizing the course. This is a great method as it allows you to test your memory before you actually run the course.

MARQ CHEEK does the following to help him memorize his course:

1. *Review map of the course.*
2. *Watch the course get built and walk the perimeter before the walk-through.*
3. *Walk the course, develop options as necessary.*
4. *Run the course (in walk-through).*
5. *Imagine the course with my eyes closed and all commands I am going to use, picturing the obstacles and where I am going to be.*
6. *Sometimes even draw the course without looking at the course or a map.*
7. *Watch the hotshots run the course and learn from them.*
8. *Watch dogs of similar size and speed. Take note of what worked and did not work.*
9. *Run the course and hope for no faults!*

Marq explains that while it is important to have a primary plan, it may be necessary to change the plan after watching other competitors. Marq says, *"I select a primary plan, but I tell myself if needed I know I can alter my plan during the run. I know I can, because I have done it before and done it successfully. I remember two of my three Super Q's in USDAA agility were runs that were never practiced in the walk-through. I invented the strategies after watching others run before me. Changing handling strategies during a run is not for everyone. People should at least be willing to change their strategy before their run if they see dog after dog go off-course as a result of handlers running the course in the same way as the handler had originally planned. It pays to go to school on others' mistakes. Close your eyes and conduct the imaginary course run and then step up to the line and nail it!"*

Clearly, Marq is also a visual learner.

NANCY GYES says that consistent practice has given her the ability to quickly memorize very challenging courses and do well. *"Much of this ability comes with practice, YEARS of it! Memorizing course after course, and being able to leave the field with a 'distinct' picture of the course and your handling strategy. It is not just the course that needs memorizing, it is the body movements between obstacles, the signals, the commands, the turns that you pattern into your mind before each run. I can still remember courses that I have run months and sometimes years before. Not all of them of course, but many of them."*

Nancy's emphasis appears to be on body movement and signaling to the dog. However, she also mentions the memorization of commands. Nancy is so successful at memorizing courses that some of them become part of her long-term memory.

ELICIA CALHOUN offers yet another approach, which begins with the course handout or tracing the course first thing in the morning. She describes her course memorization routine like this:

1. *Get handout or trace course. Analyze all different possibilities of how the course could be built and then analyze all the best ways to handle.*
2. *Watch the judge as the course is built and tweaked. As the judge tweaks, begin deciding on handling strategies.*
3. *Watch the judge measure course and analyze what sections the judge intends to be a challenge.*
4. *Walk course for the first time and walk the dog's path. Keep checking what the dog will see.*
5. *Walk course for the second time and walk the handling path.*
6. *Decide where to set dog at start line and consider what the dog will see.*
7. *Run the course as if your dog is with you and begin patterning the timing and movement necessary to successfully run the course.*
8. *Visualize your body running the course as you watch yourself from outside the ring.*
9. *Get dog and begin warming up and call all obstacles while running and playing with the dog.*
10. *Go to practice jump and imitate what is in the ring. Use this to show the dog pieces of what is in the ring.*
11. *Play the 'Ready? Ready?' game and do a sit, then down, then tug; keep the dog guessing as to what will happen after the 'Ready? Ready?'*
12. *Place dog at start line and get dog to sing with excitement.*

LINDA MECKLENBURG says, *"When I walk a course, I first learn the numerical sequence of the obstacles, identifying potential problems along the way. Then I focus on the problem areas. I weigh the risks and benefits of each potential handling maneuver based on my goals for the class (i.e., take a chance and be fast or be conservative and be clean) and my dog's strengths and weaknesses."*

Linda goes on to say, *"Once I have determined what I think is best for each dog, I walk the footwork required in the problem areas as many times as the walk-through will allow. I try to 'imprint' the steps on my short-term memory and will practice to the point where I can do it with my eyes closed. If I can do it with my eyes closed, I know I can do it while running the course with my eyes on my dog. Particularly if a cross in front is required, I want to be able to perform whatever handling maneuver I have planned without having to look for the obstacles. I should KNOW where they are."*

Ultimately, trial and error in actual competition and at matches will teach you the ideal memorization strategy for you. But there is a lot that you can do to improve course memorization before you get to competition.

## Ensure Good Memorization

Would you like to be able to look at a course and instantly memorize it and be able to recall it whenever you desire? Be careful what you ask for. Total recall would be a terrible thing. Forgetting is good. Forgetting enables you to make room for the new stuff that you need to memorize.

What agility handlers really want is *temporary* total recall. We want to be able to perfectly recall a course when we need to and then forget about it.

Steve Moidel, a memory expert, says there are some basic steps that you can take to ensure good memorization.

1. **Remember things in a unique way.** Your mind has a much easier time recalling unique things than mundane things. To use this in course memorization, try to focus on the differences and colors of equipment rather than just calling everything a jump.

2. **Use the primacy and recency effect.** When you memorize a course, it is usually very simple to memorize the opening and closing sequences. Rarely do you go off-course at the second or third obstacle, or at the second to last obstacle. This is because of the primacy and recency effect, which dictates that people memorize the beginning and the end of any type of list the best. A sequence of agility obstacles is nothing more than a list. Consequently, you are better able to absorb the parts of the obstacle sequence that you see first and last. It is the stuff in the middle that gets mixed up.

   Guard against this effect by breaking the course down into sections. This creates several beginnings and endings, thus creating more obstacles that will be easier for you to remember. The longer the course the more sections you create. Next practice memorizing each section and then chain all the sections together.

3. **Use the 7 units (+ or − 2) rule.** Short-term memory is excellent at remembering 7 units, plus or minus 2 units. This means that for most people memorizing 5–9 units is going to be the easiest to recall. Our telephone numbers are seven digits because most people can remember that many numbers. So how does that help you in agility where you mostly memorize courses with more than seven obstacles? You can apply this memorization technique easily by, again, breaking the course down into sections. A 15-obstacle course becomes three sections and you are now memorizing five obstacles at a time instead of 15.

   When competitors like Nancy Gyes report still being able to recall courses that they ran years or months ago, they have passed the information of that course from short-term memory to long-term memory. This happens because of the intensity and effectiveness of Nancy's memorization process. But if this always happened, Nancy would find herself lost on the course she is attempting to run right now, because her mind would be cluttered with old courses and unable to distinguish between the new course and some of the old courses.

4. **Attitude.** Moidel recommends that you must have the attitude that you have good course memorization skills, otherwise you are sabotaging your memory skills. Rather than memorizing the course you will be distracted by worry, because you think of yourself as having a bad memory.

5. **Attention.** Next Moidel recommends attention to what you are trying to do. Basically, there are two types of distractions that can interfere with your attention: internal and external. *Internal distraction* is more difficult to deal with. Say that while walking the course you become overly worried about a crossing pattern. Gradually you become convinced that you are likely to go off-course at the crossing pattern, because you think that you will not be able to recall which way to turn the second time you enter the pattern. You have successfully diverted your attention and now have greatly increased the likelihood of going off-course. (The Thought Power chapter of this book discussed preventing negative thoughts.) Use thought power to eliminate internal distractions.

   The *external distractions* are much easier to overcome. Make sure you are physically comfortable while walking the course. If you have to use the bathroom, use it! Do not wait until after you walked the course. Make sure you are not hungry or thirsty while walking the course. Avoid other competitors who might be distracting to you. Be organized. Have your course map handy at all times. Carry a clipboard and pencil with you for making notes. Increase your attention by implementing the strategies listed in the Focus chapter of this book.

6. **Interest.** Make sure you are motivated and interested in successfully memorizing this course. If interest is lacking, you will lack the motivation you need to make the course stick in your mind.

7. **Relaxation.** This is an integral part of good memorization. If you are overly tense and holding your breath, research shows that your memory is affected by it. Use the techniques in the Relax chapter of this book to improve your relaxation.

8. **Repetition.** Finally, Moidel recommends repetition. The more times you can repeat walking the course, the more likely that you will perfectly recall it. If you are in a competition and either miss part of the walk-through or are only given a few minutes, consider going to a quiet area on the show grounds and walking the course on plain grass. Use a sweater to mark the start line and a leash to mark the finish, and walk.

## Course Memorization Strategies

Below are strategies for you to experiment with. Use those that work for you. Make sure to try all of the strategies so that you know which ones work best for you.

1.  Memorize each individual obstacle in numerical order.

2.  Memorize sequences of obstacles that combine as an entire course.

3.  Memorize the last obstacle first and then backchain from there. With a 12-obstacle course this would be: memorizing obstacle #12, then #11 and #12, then #10, #11, and #12, and so on until you have the entire course memorized. The advantage of this approach is that you get a lot of repetition of the last half of the course. If that is a problem area for you, consider this method.

4.  Visualize the course in sequence.

5.  Write down every verbal command you are planning to give and practice repeating the commands. Focus on timing and pauses between the commands. Try to get a rhythm of the commands so that they will flow out of you when you run your dog. This works well for the auditory learner.

6.  Stand around the ring and watch others running the course from all four sides of the ring. You can also use visualization to see yourself running the course with your dog from different perspectives. You can use the visualization to speed up the course or slow it down. Some competitors find it helpful to visualize the run in fast forward, finding that this helps them feel that they have plenty of time when actually running the dog. This works well for the visual learner.

7.  Focus on memorizing your movements. You can rehearse the entire course with the movements that you plan to make. If you combine this with visualization and there is a large outdoor area, you can even run the pattern of the course and complete all the handling movements as if you were actually running your dog. This will assist you in memorizing your movements and body position through the course. Think of yourself as a dancer who is completing the judge's choreographed routine. This works well for the kinesthetic learner.

No matter what your learning style is, you must be relaxed. If you are tense, your memory is much less likely to cooperate. Nancy Gyes describes how she relaxes before a run. This enables her to both attain recall of the course she is running and build confidence.

All competitors can benefit from reviewing course diagrams. Keep all the courses that are given to you, or that you trace after they have been posted. Practice memorizing them periodically. Reading courses is a great help in

NANCY GYES uses the technique of visualizing the course in sequence. She says that she uses visualization to *"run the course a few times in my mind without looking at the field, and being able to hold that distinct picture of the course and the elements required gives me the confidence to go out and attack the run."*

Nancy says, *"If I have plenty of time before my class, I take a long walk with my dog, and get away from the main show site if possible. It clears my brain, and lets me just spend some quiet time relaxing with my teammate before we get to the job at hand. The more prepared I am for the run mentally and physically, the less inclined I am to have my nerves take control. If there are elements of the course I am still worried about, I try to visualize having a smooth and flowing run and forget about the small details. I remind myself that I am in the driver's seat and my dog is well trained. If I stay out of his way and trust him to do the job he knows, we often come out in the ribbons."*

conditioning your memory muscle. When you attend shows, save your course sheet. Then at home make a copy and practice tracing your dog's path and your handling path on the sheet. This will help develop your handling strategy skills and free up more energy for memorizing.

> A good course memorization technique creates confidence. An example of this is described by DIANE TOSH, *"I was confident about my courses because I studied them thoroughly before I walked the course. I not only studied and planned on paper, I walked the course many times, especially the problem areas. Also, I watched lots of runs before me. I could have practically run the course with my eyes closed. Because of that, I felt super confident, which in turn gave my dog confidence."*

### Memorizing Jumpers Courses

One of the most challenging courses to remember is the Jumpers course. Ask any competitor, a Jumpers course of the highest level with many crossing patterns is likely to be the biggest challenge when it comes to memorization. Competitors can practice memorizing Jumpers courses by using the colors of obstacles as a guide.

One competitor told me that she had memorized the closing sequence of a tough Jumpers course using the colors of the obstacles. As she came to the closing sequence, she knew it was the yellow double, the blue jump followed by the purple jump. This competitor had worked so hard at memorizing the colors that as she ran the closing sequence with her dog, she shouted "purple" when her dog approached the last jump. The crowd and the judge laughed, as did the competitor, and the dog, focusing on the handler's body language, cleared the jump just fine.

This competitor had branded into her memory the colors of the obstacles so distinctly that when she actually ran the course what she recalled best were the colors. If you use colors to memorize courses, make sure to practice saying the commands that you will be calling rather than repeating the colors of the obstacles to yourself over and over again. Repeating the colors may cause a problem, especially if your dog is trained to respond to verbal commands over body language.

Another technique that can assist you in memorizing Jumpers courses is memorizing the patterns. Keep in mind that in upper-level Jumpers courses you will encounter crossing patterns. Make sure you have a tried-and-true method that is effective in helping you memorize crossing patterns.

### Memorizing Crossing Patterns

One of the challenges of memorizing a course can lie in the ability to memorize crossing patterns, specifically those patterns that require you to cross paths at the same obstacle. For example, if you are required to handle the dog over a certain jump at three different times during the same course, it can be challenging to memorize when to turn in which direction. Monica Percival recommends memorizing the directions.

### Example

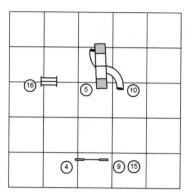

**Figure 1:** You are required to cross the same spot three times but each time you must turn the dog in a different direction. The first time you enter the sequence, you will go straight over the A-frame. The second time, you will navigate your dog to the tunnel to the right, and the third time to the triple bar jump to the left. Monica would memorize this pattern as jump then straight, jump then right, and jump then left. This is a great simplification over attempting to memorize the pattern this sequence creates.

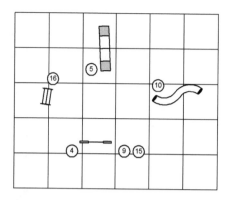

**Figure 2:** You can apply the same principle for memorizing a similar pattern in which the obstacles are further apart as in this sequence. However, you can still use Monica's memorization strategy of straight, right, and left.

## If You Run More Than One Dog

When running multiple dogs in the same class you essentially have two options. The first is that you handle both dogs exactly the same way. If you choose this option, you will want to plan your handling strategy for the best dog. Your second option is to handle the course differently for each dog. If you choose option two, you may want to spend a significant amount of time practicing running the dogs and having to shift your strategies. The only way that you will complete option two successfully is if you practice it just how it will be in competition.

## Memorizing More than One Course

Stuart Mah has a great technique for memorizing two courses at the same time. Stuart recommends walking first the course that you will run second. Walk this course, develop your strategy, and then forget it. Clear your mind and now begin walking the second course, which you will run first. This way the course you walked last is the first one you run and therefore is fresh in your mind. Since course memorization is short-term memory, you do not want to clutter your mind with attempting to memorize two courses at once. When you have completed your first run, go back and start watching the other competitors running your next course. This will refresh your memory.

An example of this would be Beth who is running her dog in both Open Jumpers with Weaves and Excellent Standard. The club putting on the show has two rings going and one class is in each ring. Beth knows that Jumpers with Weaves is going faster, so she will run Jumpers before Standard. Because of this Beth begins with walking the Excellent Standard course. When she is comfortable with her strategy and has memorized the course, she clears her mind and heads for the second ring. At the second ring she memorizes her Jumpers course and then proceeds to run it successfully. She quickly plays with her dog to reward his good performance and then begins to watch the Excellent Standard runs. By watching the runs, her memory is refreshed and she is ready to go!

### Final Ideas on Course Memorization

- Read Stuart Mah's book *Fundamentals of Course Design for Dog Agility*. This excellent book describes course design in detail. Memorization improves when you understand more about courses and how they are put together.

- Consider buying obstacle miniatures and setting up miniature courses specifically of those courses you have had trouble memorizing. Then have a miniature dog run the course with you as the handler. Course miniatures are available from Kelly McIntosh at (904) 282-7998 or from MAX 200 at (800) 446-2920.

- Another helpful tool to help you practice memorizing courses are magnetic course boards. You arrange pre-cut magnetic obstacles on a magnetic board so that you can copy courses from the posted course at a show or create your own courses. Set up a course on the board and then practice memorizing it. Clean Run Productions sells magnetic course boards. You can see the boards on their web site at www.cleanrun.com. You can also reach them at (800) 311-6503.

No matter which tool you choose, it will be important to practice. Practice is what will give you the memory and the recall that you desire.

# Questions to Ask Yourself

Take a moment to review the memorization strategies that could be helpful to you. Remember that all strategies must be tested and proven before being used in competition.

| | |
|---|---|
| **1. My course memorization strategy is going to be** | |
| **2. In the past, I have had a hard time memorizing (list sequences or types of courses)** | |
| **3. In the future, I plan to take the following steps to prevent the memorization problems with the sequences or type of courses listed above:** | |

## Chapter 13

# In Conclusion

*"Believe in yourself and in your dog. (And do your homework, so you have reason to believe in yourself and your dog!) Eat and drink properly. Love the course. Avoid people who are whining or worrying. Internalize only what is good for you. Visualize what you DO want, including the entirety of your perfect run in detail. Breathe. Loosen up yourself and your dog. Know and do what helps your dog when you are on deck. Go for it!"*

—Julie Daniels

If you think you would like additional assistance with getting into and staying in the Zone consider the following:

- Go through this workbook again six months from now. Sometimes you can only get so much out of material you are reading, and later you will be able to take in more.
- Keep a Zone journal.

If you keep a Zone journal, keep track of what was happening when you Zoned. What happened the day of the competition? What was different? What had you eaten? What had you done with your dog? Had you gotten a lot of sleep or barely any? Getting barely any sleep might indicate that you were operating on adrenaline. You could recreate the adrenaline rush without sleep deprivation and probably do even better. How did you memorize/analyze the course?

The journal needs to comprehensively list everything that could be a factor in getting you and your dog into the Zone. Use this book to help you to create a list of your personal Zone factors. The factors listed would be all activities that help get you into the Zone.

Some Zone factors are listed below. Use these categories as a guideline for your Zone journal.

- Anything you do in preparation for competition
- Games you play with your dog

- Whom you socialize with
- What you ate and drank
- What you are feeding your dog
- How much and where you slept
- Your physical conditioning
- Your dog's conditioning
- What you are doing to keep your confidence where it needs to be
- What you are thinking
- Your skills in terms of keeping yourself focused on the task at hand
- What you visualize
- What you do to relax yourself and your dog
- How you keep pressure from impacting you in a negative way
- How you energize yourself or your dog
- Your macro and micro pre-competition rituals

When you have gathered all the information in your journal, simply do more of what works and less or none of what does not work.

Use the competition worksheet on the following page to gather additional information.

## Competition Worksheet

### *Event Information*

Dates:

Organization:

Indoor/Outdoor:

Weather conditions:

Ring conditions:

Type of facility:

Footing:

Number of runs:

List of runs including class, time, score, and placement:

### *Dog Information*

Physical condition of dog:

Mood of dog:

What dog ate and drank:

How much rest dog had:

Dog's reaction to show site:

Dog's reaction to equipment:

Brief description of dog's attitude during run:

How was the dog's focus?

What relaxation technique did you use to assist the dog in resting?

What energizing technique did you use?

Other information:

## Handler Information

Your physical condition:

Your mood:

What did you eat and drink:

How much sleep did you have the night before competition?

Did you nap?

What was your reaction to the show site:

What thoughts or comments assisted your performance:

What thoughts or comments restricted your performance:

How was your focus?

What did you visualize?

What relaxation exercises did you use?

What energizing exercises did you use?

What, if anything, happened that caused you to feel pressured?

Other information:

## Interaction with the Dog

How much did you play with your dog and at what times?

What games did you play with your dog?

How much fun do you think the dog had?

Other information:

## Action Plan

What changes do you need to make for the dog to Zone?

What changes do you need to make for you to Zone?

Other ideas:

In addition to this competition worksheet, you might want to develop a list of what works when you realize that you are overaroused or underaroused. When you are at competition and you notice that you are overaroused, you can conveniently check your list of things to do and pick from it.

When I am overaroused it helps to (check the chapters on Relaxation, Visualization, Confidence for ideas)

> (blank box)

When I am underaroused it helps to (check the Energizing chapter for ideas)

> (blank box)

For several trials, fill out a competition worksheet. Compare the days of the competition to each other, but also compare separate trials to each other. Use all of this information to find patterns. What you are looking for are things like usually doing better on Sunday than on Saturday. Then explore the reasons why you are doing better on Sunday. Have you and your dog adjusted to the environment? Have your nerves worn off? Use the information that you discover to tweak the system. If you do better on Sundays, explore what is happening on that day and work to duplicate it on Saturdays. If your nerves wear off on the second day, consider familiarizing yourself with the show site the night before or by going to matches that are at locations with which you are unfamiliar.

1. Gather the information.
2. Look for patterns.
3. Understand why the patterns are occurring.
4. Tweak the system.

## The Elements of Zoning

The chapters of this book represent elements of what will help you reach your peak performance Zone. For each element, there are many tools. Take a final look at each chapter and the tools presented. Which ones do you plan on using?

❑ Goal Setting for the Zone
❑ Confidence
❑ Thought Power

❑ Focus

❑ Visualize

❑ Relax

❑ Energizing

❑ Overlearning

❑ Competition

All of these tools can help make the difference in your relationship with your dog, your attitude, and your performance.

Congratulations, by completing this book and implementing what you have learned, you are taking the first steps necessary to enter the agility success Zone!

# Top Competitor Biographies

### Ken Boyd

Ken and his dog Becky started taking agility classes in June of 1994. Their first competition was a NADAC trial in November of 1994. This was the beginning of a very successful agility team. Since then Becky has earned the following titles: MX and MXJ in AKC, NATCH in NADAC, and ADCH in USDAA.

At the 1996 USDAA Grand Prix Nationals in Ventura, CA, Becky took 6th in Time Gamble, 6th in Jumpers, and 6th in Three-Dog Relay (with Kathie Leggett's Spirit and Nancy Fairchild's Rosie). At the 1996 AKC Nationals in Gutherie, OK, Becky placed 3rd in round one and 4th in round four. Overall, Becky and Ken finished one spot away from last place, but they *"had a blast"* and were *"just toenails away from finishing much higher."*

In 1997, Ken and Becky became the first dog and handler team to win the Triple Crown of dog agility. They did this by winning the National Championship in all three agility organizations:

- USDAA: Grand Prix National Champion in the 12-inch division in Cleveland, OH.

- NADAC: National Champion in the Overall Competition in the 12-inch Elite Class in Scottsdale, AZ. In addition, Becky placed 1st in 12-inch Elite Jumpers, 1st in 12-inch Elite Gamblers, and was the high-scoring 12-inch Elite dog on the second day.

- AKC: National Champion in the 12-inch class in Chicago, IL. In addition, Becky placed 1st in round one, 4th in round two, 6th in round three, and 3rd in the final round.

### Elicia Calhoun

Elicia is a top national competitor and trainer, and a newly certified USDAA judge. She and her Australian Shepherd, Suni, were members of the 1999 AKC World Team representing the U.S. in Dortmund, Germany at the World Agility Championships. Elicia has placed in the top 10 at the 1998 AKC, NADAC, and USDAA National Championships and has been in the

USDAA Agility Top Ten since 1996. She was shown competing on the television network Animal Planet several times in 1998 and 1999, and on ESPN in 1999 for the Purina Incredible Dog Challenge Competition.

Elicia is a full-time dog trainer who travels across the country competing and giving seminars, and teaches local group classes/private lessons in New Jersey for dog and handler teams of all ages and levels. She owns three dogs:

- Jettie, a recently retired 8-year-old Lab/Greyhound Mix, began competing in 1994 and finished her ADCH title within two years. She was ranked in USDAA's Agility Top Ten for 1996 and 1997.

- Suni, a 4-year-old Australian Shepherd and Elicia's newest competition dog, made her agility debut in April of 1997 and earned her ADCH title within the first nine months of competition. She was ranked in USDAA's Agility Top Ten for 1997 and 1998. Suni currently competes at the USDAA Masters, AKC Excellent, and NADAC Elite Levels.

- Leg-O, a 3-year-old mixed breed, has limited competition prospects because she lost her front left leg at eight weeks of age. She does, however, herd sheep. She also earned her CGC and placed 5th in the Tunnelers game at the 1998 NADAC Nationals.

### Marquand Cheek

Marq is an AKC judge, a 1998 AKC Agility Advisory Panel Member, an AKC/USDAA competitor, and an occasional columnist for *Clean Run* magazine. Additionally, he has instructed at agility training camps and conducts a light seminar circuit of his own. He has earned the AKC MX and MXJ titles on his Sheltie, Thomas, as well as herding and obedience titles. His other Sheltie, Wyatt, earned his USDAA ADCH title before he was three and finished 3rd at the 1998 USDAA Grand Prix National Championships. Wyatt also finished in USDAA's Agility Top Ten in all four categories in 1998. In June of 1999 Wyatt and Marq became the first team to capture the AKC MACH (Master Agility Champion) title. He and his dog placed 4th in national Sheltie AKC agility standings for 1997 and led the standings for 1999.

### Julie Daniels

Julie has many titles and wins with five dogs, including two Rottweilers, an English Springer Spaniel, a Border Collie, and a Cairn Terrier. She has been a USDAA Grand Prix semi-finalist 11 years in a row, and is a 6-time finalist. In 1997 and 1998 she was lead commentator at the USDAA Nationals for the Animal Planet TV network. She is the author of *Enjoying Dog Agility*, and co-author of *Jumping From A to Z*. In addition, she has been a columnist for *Clean Run* magazine and *The Clicker Journal*. Julie is the owner of White Mountain Agility School in New Hampshire, and founder of the five-day Agility Instructor Certification Course and the Competition Camp. She conducts seminars in agility and clicker training at all levels.

### Susan Garrett

Susan trains and competes in agility simply because she and her dogs love the sport. All three of her dogs possess a collection of "gold cups" won at both the regional and national level. Impressive highlights of her dogs' agility careers include:

• Stoni, an 8-year-old Border Collie, was the USDAA Grand Prix National Champion in both 1996 and 1998, making her one of the very few dogs to have won this competition twice. Stoni has also placed everywhere from 4th to 1st at the Dog Agility Masters team finals and she won the 1999 national Agility Steeplechase finals. This makes Stoni the only dog to have won all three of the USDAA agility tournaments.

• Shelby, Susan's 11-year-old Jack Russell Terrier, was the 8-inch Champion at the 1997 Pup-Peroni Agility Classic. The following year Shelby won both the USDAA Grand Prix Nationals and the NADAC National Championships.

• Twister, a blistering fast 6-year-old Jack Russell, was the 1998 NADAC National Champion in the 12-inch division and has won many individual trophies at various National Championships.

In 1998, Susan became the only handler ever to win two divisions in the same year at a National Championship. Astoundingly, she did this not once but twice in the same year. She won the USDAA Grand Prix in the 12-inch and 24-inch divisions with Shelby and Stoni. Later that autumn, she followed this by winning the NADAC Nationals in the 8-inch and 12-inch classes with Shelby and Twister.

In addition to the success they have in agility, Stoni and Twister also run on the team that currently holds the world record in flyball (16.06 seconds!). Are you getting goose bumps?

Susan's newest dog, 2-year-old Buzz, is familiar to many *Clean Run* magazine readers through a monthly column called, "What's the Buzz", which described the trials and tribulations of living with a high-drive Border Collie.

Susan lives in Ancaster, Ontario, Canada with her partner, John Blenkey, and owns and operates Say Yes Dog Training. Say Yes emphasizes clicker and play-training as the foundation of all instruction. Susan is in great demand as a seminar leader, and has taught throughout Canada, the U.S., Japan, and England on the use of clicker training for agility, flyball, and competition obedience.

### Katie Greer

Katie started out in agility in 1991 with the Dallas Agility Working Group. She taught classes, held various offices, and gave seminars. She is a former AKC judge, and has written for several publications, including *Agility Spotlight* and *Clean Run* magazine. She was a member of the ASCA Agility Committee from 1993 until October of 1997. In November of 1997 she started working as a Field Representative for the AKC Agility Department.

Katie's dogs' titles include: ADCH Annie Mo Bannie FDCH, All-American; Chelsea Roux MAD, JM, RM, CD, retired Labrador Retriever; ADCH Lace MX, Australian Shepherd; Samson AAD, OA, Chihuahua. Katie continues to compete in USDAA and judges outside the U.S. In 1999 Katie judged agility at the World Dog Show in Mexico City.

### Nancy Gyes

Nancy operates Power Paws Agility, one of the largest and most successful dog agility training schools in the country. She and many of her students have earned top titles in all the major sanctioning organizations. She has been involved in teaching and participating in dog sports (obedience, tracking, and breeding) for over 17 years. She has been training and competing in agility for 8 years and is best known for her Border Collie, Scud, who has earned the USDAA ADCH title; the AKC MX, MXJ, and CDX titles; and all NADAC Elite titles. Nancy and Scud were and are members of all four of the AKC-sponsored U.S. teams that competed at the 1996, 1997, 1998, and 1999 World Agility Championships in Switzerland, Denmark, Slovenia, and Germany, respectively. She has put USDAA ADCH titles on five dogs: Scud, Riot, and Wicked, Border Collies; and her two mixed breeds, Toast and Winston. Nancy and her dogs have made seven appearances in the USDAA National Finals. Notable placements have been: Scud, finished 2nd in 1995 and 1997, and won the 30-inch division 1998. Riot finished 2nd in 1998 and won the 22-inch division in 1999.

Nancy is recognized as one of the top trainers and competitors in the sport, and travels throughout the country competing and giving seminars. She is dedicated to furthering her own knowledge of the sport, by both hosting other top trainers from England and North America, and traveling to other parts of the world to work with the top trainers in the sport.

### Pati Hatfield

Although only active in dog agility since 1994, Pati and her Belgian Malinois, Lilly, have become one of the top teams competing in the sport. Pati and Lilly were selected as members of the AKC World Agility Team in both 1996 and 1997, representing the United States in international competition in Switzerland and Denmark. Pati and Lilly won the 1997 USDAA Grand Prix Nationals 30-inch division and had the fastest time of all jump heights. Pati and Lilly were also members of the winning team at the 1997 USDAA Dog Agility Masters Tournament in Fairhill, MD. In 1999, Pati and Lilly placed 2nd in the 26-inch division at the USDAA Grand Prix Nationals.

Pati's extensive background in behavioral training and modifying problem behavior in dogs has contributed to her success in helping other dog/handler teams meet their agility goals. Pati works with a variety of breeds and enjoys developing each dog to his own potential. Pati's training programs emphasize solid basics combined with an enjoyable working relationship between dog and handler.

Her dog Lilly has earned the following titles: CH (AKC breed champion with three 5-point majors in one weekend), U-AG II, ADCH, MX, MXJ, CDX, and NJC.

### Bud Houston

Bud has been instrumental to the sport of dog agility. He began publishing *Clean Run*, a dog agility publication, in 1995. This magazine is the best agility publication available today and has significantly influenced the growth and direction of agility in the U.S. Bud retired from the magazine in 1999 to focus on his training business.

Bud's Shelties have attained such titles as the elusive ADCH, MAD, and many others. Bud is also a judge for AKC and USDAA, and operates the agility training camp called Camp Dogwood.

### Mindy Lytle

Mindy is a professional artist who paints murals. Her Jack Russell Terrier, Westwood Zoe, has her ADCH, AG-I, AG-II, all titles at the NADAC Elite level, and the AKC MX and MXJ titles. Zoe was a finalist (8th place) in the 1997 USDAA Grand Prix Nationals 12-inch division, a semi-finalist in 1998 USDAA Grand Prix Nationals, and in 1999 she was again a finalist and got 6th place in the 12-inch division.

Mindy began competing in agility four years ago in what was then called NCDA and is now known as UKC agility. Mindy also competed in Jack Russell Terrier competitions, qualifying and placing in the national competition many times. Mindy makes it a point to keep all the negatives out of Zoe's training and wishes she had known about clicker training when Zoe was eight weeks old. Mindy's motto is: "There is nothing like a fast clean run!"

### Stuart Mah

Stuart Mah began his agility training career in 1989. His first dog, Shannon UD, HC, EAC, ADCH, an All-American, was a member of the U.S. Agility Team that competed in Germany in 1991 and Spain in 1992. Shannon has competed in the USDAA Grand Prix Finals four times with placements in the top six each time, including a win in 1991 and two bronze placements in 1993 and 1994. Shannon was elected to the USDAA Agility Hall of Fame in 1991 and is now in semi-retirement after attaining her ADCH title in 1995 at the age of 10. Stuart is currently competing in agility with Recce, MX, MXJ, ADCH, a Border Collie. Recce's accomplishments include a top-four placement in the 1994 USDAA Grand Prix Finals and a win at the 1998 AKC Nationals. Stuart and Recce were members of four U.S. Agility Teams: 1995 in Belgium, 1996 in Switzerland, 1998 in Slovenia, and 1999 in Germany.

Stuart has been teaching since 1992. His students have gained top honors in national competition and have attained numerous agility titles in all flavors of the sport. He has given seminars on agility training nationwide and is licensed to judge agility for every major agility organization in the U.S. and Canada.

Stuart was inducted into the USDAA Agility Hall of Fame in 1991 and was also selected "Agility Person of the Year" in 1995. He is the author of several books including *Fundamentals of Course Design for Dog Agility*, *A Correspondence Course for Agility Course Design* (with Linda Mecklenburg), and *The Clean Run Book of Agility Games* (with Bud Houston). He has also written numerous articles for *Clean Run* magazine, *USDAA Agility Report*, *Southern California Dog Magazine*, and the *Agility Spotlight*.

### Linda Mecklenburg

Linda has represented the U.S. in international competition on five occasions (twice with the USDAA at the Pedigree World Cup and three times with the AKC at the World Championships). She is the only handler, thus far, to have competed with two different dogs at the World Championships. Linda has been a USDAA Grand Prix National finalist five years in a row, and in 1997 handled her dog Spiffy to the 24-inch Championship. Her dogs, Nifty and Spiffy, have both been ranked in the Top Ten in AKC agility (*Front and Finish*) for the last three years and one or the other has been the number one Border Collie each year. In 1996, Nifty was ranked the number one dog All-Breed in AKC agility. In 1998, Spiffy was ranked number one. Linda has handled five dogs to both the USDAA MAD and the AKC MX titles, including her four Border Collies and Sue Klar's Pembroke Welsh Corgi, Kayla.

Four of Linda's dogs have the USDAA ADCH title. Linda was a member of the USDAA National DAM Champion Team in 1995 and 1997, and her dogs have been on the USDAA Top Ten lists every year. She recently added a new member to her pack, a bi-black Sheltie named Marvel. Watch for him in 2001! Linda is co-owner of Clean Run Productions, a company that publishes the monthly agility magazine *Clean Run* as well as a variety of agility training books.

### Monica Percival

Known as one of the top agility competitors in the Northeast since she started competing with her English Springer Spaniels in 1990, Monica has also enjoyed success at the national level. Monica is a nine-time semi-finalist in the USDAA Grand Prix Nationals and was a finalist with her Border Collie, Lazer, in 1998. In qualifying for the USDAA Nationals, her dogs have won five Grand Prix Regional Qualifers and have placed in the top three multiple times. Monica and Lazer won the national USDAA Dog Agility Steeplechase finals in both 1997 and 1999. They have also earned multiple placements in individual classes at USDAA national tournaments. (At only two years of age, Lazer won the Gamblers class at both the USDAA Grand Prix Nationals and the DAM Team Tournament Nationals with the highest score in all height categories out of more than 200 dogs.) In 1998, Lazer won the 24-inch division at the NADAC Nationals and captured a 3rd place in the 1999 NADAC Nationals with a borrowed handler. He was also the winner of the 1999 Eastern region Purina Incredible Dog Challenge televised by ESPN and took 4th place in the national finals. Lazer started showing in AKC agility in late fall of 1998, and just one year later finished in 13th place at the 1999 AKC Nationals. He has earned his USDAA ADCH, AKC AX and AXJ, and NADAC Open titles, and was in the USDAA Agility Top Ten in the 30-inch division in all categories in both 1996 and 1997.

Monica's All-American, Boomer, is working at the USDAA Masters level. The Springers have all been retired.

Monica has been an instructor at more than 20 dog training camps and has conducted seminars around the U.S. and in Canada. In addition to competing and teaching, Monica founded Pipe Dreams, the first company in the U.S. to manufacture agility equipment and is the inventor of the infamous "Weave-A-Matic." Monica is co-owner of Clean Run Productions, a company that publishes the monthly agility magazine *Clean Run* as well as a variety of agility training books.

### Jane Simmons-Moake

Jane is one of the world's foremost agility trainers. A top-winning competitor, veteran judge, and award-winning author, Jane runs one of the nation's most successful agility training organizations, FlashPaws Agility Training Center. A popular seminar leader in the U.S. and abroad, Jane has also competed internationally as a member of the 1996 and 1997 U.S. Agility Teams. Jane has also authored an award-winning three-tape video series on how to teach your dog competitive agility and has authored two books: *Agility Training* and *Excelling at Dog Agility*.

### Diane Tosh

Diane has been competing in agility since 1993. She is a competitor and dedicated instructor. She uses operant conditioning and proactive behavioral methods in her training. Diane draws heavily from learning theory when instructing her students on how to better teach their dogs the behaviors that they desire. Diane is currently preparing her young Border Collie, Gretsky, to compete. Diane's Jack Russell Terrier, Petey, was one of the first Jack Russells in the country to receive his AX in AKC. He qualified and successfully competed at AKC Nationals in 1998. Petey has also been ranked in the USDAA Agility Top Ten.

# Sources and Recommended Reading

### Books or Tapes on Psychology

*The Psychology of Winning* by Denis Waitley. New York: Berkley Book, 1979. This is an important book on motivation.

*That Winning Feeling!* by Jane Savoie. Vermont: Trafalgar Square Publishing, 1992. An equestrian book about mental competition skills.

*The Achievement Zone* by Shane Murphy, Ph.D. New York: G.P. Putnam's Sons, 1996. Murphy assists the reader in achieving success regardless of your goal.

*Mental Training for Peak Performance* by Steven Ungerleider, Ph.D. Pennsylvania: Rodale Press, Inc., 1996. Sports psychology including stories of world-class athletes.

*Sports Psyching* by Thomas Tutko, Ph.D. and Umberto Tosi. New York: G.P. Putnam's Sons, 1976. Sports psychology to assist you to "play your best game all the time."

*Stop Setting Goals: If You Would Rather Solve Problems* by Bob Biehl. New York: Random House, 1995. This book is out of print. Biehl argues that goal setting is not for everyone.

*Heads Up!* by Janet Sasson Edgette, Psy.D. New York: Doubleday, 1996. A book about mental competition skills written by a psychologist who is also an equestrian.

*Flow* by Mihaly Csikszentmihalyi. New York: HarperCollins, 1990. Csikszentmihalyi coined the term "flow." Flow is also commonly referred to as "the Zone." This book talks about every aspect of flow you could possibly think of.

*The New Toughness Training for Sports* by James E. Loehr, Ed.D. New York: Penguin Books, 1994. Loehr emphasizes becoming tough mentally and physically to prepare for top competition.

*Exploring Sport and Exercise Psychology* by Judy L. Van Raalte and Britton W. Brewer (Editors). Washington, DC: American Psychological Association, 1996. This is an academic book emphasizing research and findings of prominent sport psychology researchers. This book is best used as a reference.

*The Twenty Minute Break* by Ernest Rossi, Ph.D. Los Angeles: Jeremy Tarcher, 1991. This book describes our natural rhythms of rest and recuperation and how they can be used to enhance performance. This book's focus is not on sports.

"Memory Power" by Steve Moidel. Careertrack, Boulder, CO, audiotape. This tape discusses in detail techniques for improving your memory.

*Feeling Good* by David D. Burns, M.D. Signet Publishers, 1981. This is an excellent book that explains how to change your thoughts to change your emotions.

"The Seven Habits of Highly Effective People" by Steven Covey. Audio tapes by Covey Leadership Center, Provo, UT. These tapes are an excellent resource on time management and organization, and on learning what makes people excel and how you can do it yourself.

*The Ten Natural Laws of Time and Life Management* by Hyrum Smith. Warner Books, New York, NY. This is an outstanding book that can increase your organizational skills. Can be applied to structuring training sessions as well as organization as a whole.

### Books or Tapes on Dog Training and Agility Training

*The Culture Clash* by Jean Donaldson. Berkeley: James & Kenneth Publishers, 1996. A must-read for anyone who trains dogs.

*Fundamentals of Course Design for Dog Agility* by Stuart Mah. Clean Run Productions, 1997. A book on course design that is written to help any competitor understand how the design of a course affects the handler's and dog's performance. Available from Clean Run Productions at www.cleanrun.com or (800) 311-6503.

*Purely Positive: Companion to Competition* by Sheila Booth. Podium Publications, 1998. This book discusses how to train your dog with non-force methods for companion obedience, competition obedience, and agility. Available from Clean Run Productions at www.cleanrun.com or (800) 311-6503.

"Positively Ringwise" by Patty Ruzzo. This audiotape is available from Dogwise at (800) 776-2665 or www.dogwise.com. Patty discusses methods the handler can use to succeed in the competition obedience ring.

"Dog Show Noise Tape", an audiotape that is available from Dogwise at (800) 776-2665 or www.dogwise.com. This tape can help adjust your dog to the noises of dog shows and reduce your dog's stress.

*Calming Signals* by Turid Rugaas. This is an interesting book. While there is no scientific evidence to back up Rugaas's claims about canine body language, this book clearly makes you think and watch your dog.

*Introductory Agility Workbook, Intermediate Agility Workbook, and Advanced Agility Workbook* by Clean Run Productions, 1997. These workbooks are great for instructors and for competitors that are trying to get a regular training schedule. Available from Clean Run Productions at www.cleanrun.com or (800) 311-6503.

"Click and Treat Video" by Gary Wilkes. A fun tape that explains the basics of clicker training. It also explains the useful process of variable reinforcement. Available from Dogwise at (800) 776-2665 or www.dogwise.com.

"Nerves to Verve" and "Clear Mind Clean Run" both are 45 minutes audiotapes and are for sale from Flying Dog Press. Call (800) 7 FLY DOG or visit their website at www.flyingdogpress.com to order. These tapes are self-hypnotic tapes that will help you relax.

"Competitive Agility Training" a series of three videotapes by Jane Simmons-Moake. These excellent tapes are a wonderful resource and are beautifully produced. Available from Clean Run Productions at www.cleanrun.com or (800) 311-6503.

*Don't Shoot the Dog!* by Karen Pryor. Bantam Books, 1985. Revised August 1999. This milestone book is a must read for anyone who wants to train her dog to do anything. Available from Dogwise at (800) 776-2665 or www.dogwise.com.

*Peak Performance: Coaching the Canine Athlete, Second Edition* by Chris Zink. Canine Sports Productions, Inc., 1997. Highly recommended reading for anyone with a competition dog. A must read for the serious agility competitor. Available from Clean Run Productions at www.cleanrun.com or (800) 311-6503.

*The Tellington Touch for Dogs* by Linda Tellington-Jones and Robyn Hood. Thane Marketing International, 1994. Available through Dogwise at (800) 776-2665 or www.dogwise.com.

*Agility Tricks* by Donna Duford. Clean Run Productions, 1999. A book on teaching tricks to dogs for improved attention, flexibility, and confidence in agility. Available from Clean Run Productions at www.cleanrun.com or (800) 311-6503.

# About the Author

**ANGELICA STEINKER, M.ED.** has a Masters degree in Counseling and Development from George Mason University in Fairfax, Virginia. She owns and operates a full-time dog training business called Courteous Canine, Inc. which provides pet obedience and agility instruction. She is married and lives near Tampa, Florida with her three Jack Russell Terriers and a Border Collie puppy. She has worked in mental health, consulting, and executive coaching.

Articles she has written have been published in *Dalmatian Quarterly, Clean Run, Captain Haggerty's The Aggression Newsletter,* and other publications.

Angelica is an AKC agility judge and competes with her dogs in AKC, NADAC, and USDAA. She is an avid clicker trainer and loves the challenge and process of shaping a behavior.

She has presented her Zone material in Vermont at Camp Gone to the Dogs.

Angelica with Moose, Junior, and Arnie.

PHOTO BY JANE LEGARD PHOTOGRAPHY

Angelica's new addition, Nicki.

PHOTO BY LYNN SICKINGER PHOTOGRAPHY.

**Let Me Hear Your Success Stories**
If you have a success story of how you conquered your show nerves or any other success, let me hear from you.
Email, fax, or send your success story to:

Angelica Steinker, M.Ed.
Courteous Canine, Inc.
2601 Spring Green Dr
Lutz, FL 33549
Email: Angelica@CourteousCanine.com
Fax: 813-949-1465